The Only Golf Lesson
You'll Ever Need

The Only Golf Lesson You'll Ever Need

Easy Solutions to Problem Golf Swings

HANK HANEY
with John Huggan

HarperCollins*Publishers*

A MOUNTAIN LION BOOK

HarperCollins books may be purchased for educational, business, or sales promotional use. For information, please write to: Special Markets Department, HarperCollins Publishers, Inc., 10 East 53rd Street, New York, New York 10022.

FIRST EDITION

Library of Congress Cataloging-in-Publication Data

Haney, Hank
      The only golf lesson you'll ever need : easy solutions to problem golf swings / Hank Haney with John Huggan. — 1st ed.
          p.   cm.
      Includes index.
      ISBN 0–06–270237–8
      1. Swing (Golf) 2. Golf—Study and teaching.   I. Huggan, John.
II. Title.
GV979.S9H28   1999
796.352'3—dc21   98–52416
                                                                                                  CIP

99 00 01 02 03 IPA/RRD 10 9 8 7 6 5 4

For my wife, Jerilynn, my biggest supporter.

Contents

Acknowledgments

My most sincere thanks to Jim Hardy, who really taught me about teaching.

To John Cleland, for giving my career its start.

To John Jacobs, the finest teacher I ever saw, for giving me the confidence to pursue my dream of being one of the best.

To Byron Nelson and the late Ben Hogan, for sending me students.

I would also like to thank my co-author John Huggan for doing such a wonderful job in transferring my thoughts onto paper, Dom Furore for his expert photography, and John Monteleone and Randy Voorhees of Mountain Lion, Inc.

Most of all, however, my gratitude goes to Mark O'Meara. Thanks for being my once in a lifetime student, bud.

Foreword

It was the fall of '82. I was in my second year on the PGA Tour and I was struggling. In fact, it looked at that point like I might lose my tour card. I had no idea what I was doing wrong. Everyone told me I had a nice swing, but I had always wondered why, if that were the case, I didn't play better. And how come I felt so bad over some shots?

Don't get me wrong. I was a pretty good player at that point. I'd won the U.S. Amateur championship, needed only one visit to the Q-school en route to the tour, and been rookie of the year in my first full season. But I was getting by on natural ability and nice rhythm. Which can be fine. Some days I played really well. But I was never consistent, especially under pressure. My philosophy was that if I hooked a shot I must have swung too fast. In other words, I was un-believably naive when it came to understanding how my swing worked—or didn't work.

Then fate took a hand.

I was on the practice range at the Pinehurst Hotel & Country Club when I bumped into a young instructor by the name of Hank Haney. Little did I know at the time that meeting Hank would be one of the most significant events in my career.

Before our first lesson I was like any other golfer—in need of a quick fix. Hank watched me hit balls for about thirty-five to forty minutes and never said a word. I kept waiting for him to tell me to move the ball forward or change my grip; the sort of things you'd typically hear from any other instructor.

Eventually Hank asked me if I had thirty minutes to go sit down and talk about what I needed to do. I thought, "Not really. I'm about to lose my card. I need to keep pounding away here."

But he said, "Nah, we're not doing any good here. Let's go talk about what I think is the correct way to swing the golf club. On the way I'll point out the way you are swinging and why you are seeing the ball-flight you've got right now."

So we did that. Hank opened my eyes to the fact that I had some major flaws in my swing. If I wanted to be more consistent, we had some work to do.

Hank convinced me that if I worked on shallowing my swing plane and getting my arms and body working as one then my impact position would be better and my ball-flight would be better. Under the gun I'd be better, too. Mental toughness can only take you so far. Over the last few holes of a tournament you need a technique you can count on.

I didn't get better right away. In fact, I got worse before I got better. Of course, it's a constant battle to improve at this game—I'm still trying to improve my technique—but Hank told me there was no time frame.

So all of a sudden I was thinking of three or four things on the course. I'd never done that before and my swing became more mechanical. So I struggled. But we worked and worked and eventually I got it.

In the last sixteen years Hank has watched me hit well over a million golf balls. There have been some trying moments but I'm glad we both hung in there. The light at the end of my particular tunnel came on at the end of '83. I won my first event in '84 at Milwaukee and finished second on the money list.

Now, that had a lot to do with me, but I know it would have been difficult to achieve the success I have without the commitment and hard work Hank has put into my game. I'm proud of the way my swing holds up in all kinds of conditions and under the severest pressure. Both are a tribute to Hank and his teaching. He knows more about ball-flight and what controls it than anyone in the game. And if you understand that, you're on your way.

What makes Hank different for me is how positive he is. He really believes in himself and his ability to make you a better golfer. And he was so willing to help me get better. Those are the things you look for in an instructor.

Indeed, that's what makes Hank such a great instructor—his willingness to help people. He's always looking for ways to help you improve.

What he's told me can help everybody. In fact, Hank gets more enjoyment out of teaching high-handicappers than he does from working with a tour pro. He can fix anyone.

People have often asked me how to describe Hank Haney. To me, he is a man on a mission. He's dedicated to being the best that he can be. He's first-class all the way and he loves golf. That is the type of person I want around me.

Today, Hank is my best friend. He has been there for me more than anyone outside of my immediate family. He's been a mentor of sorts, too. He has helped me with every aspect of my game, not just my full swing.

Hank also has the ability to laugh. We were practicing at Pinehurst one time. It was raining. The temperature was barely above freezing. And our session wasn't going well. I started with my sand wedge and that wasn't going right. So I threw it down the range. Then I went to my wedge. Same thing. And so on right through the bag. Eventually all I had left was my umbrella and my golf bag. All Hank said was, "Well, we could work with the umbrella, but now might be a good time to take a little break."

We went in, had a drink, and came back out. Then we started over. Hank would stand there and watch me hit all day. That's the sort of commitment he has to all of his pupils. He's a special man and a great teacher.

Even today, twenty-odd tournament wins and two professional major championship victories later, there are still flaws in my swing. Hank and I know that. But we're still working to get better. Now you've found him, too. Read on and improve.

MARK O'MEARA
JULY 1998

Part One

Understanding Your Swing

1

Where I'm Coming From
The Learning Sequence

Hi, I'm Hank Haney. Thanks for coming to me for a golf lesson. Before I take a look at your swing and your shots, let me ask a few questions about you and your game.

How long have you played golf?
What is your handicap?
What is the lowest your handicap has ever been?
How often do you play?
How often do you practice?
Where does your ball go? Does it slice? Does it hook?
Where do most of your short-iron shots finish?
Do you tend to hit the ball fat or thin?
When you hit it fat, do you make a deep divot, or simply hit behind the ball?
Do you tend to hit the ball off the toe of the club, or the heel of the club?
Do your shots tend to start right of your target, or left of your target?
Do your shots tend to fly too high or too low?
Which shot gives you the most difficulty?
What is your favorite club?
What is your least favorite club?
If you had a tree in your way and could play either a slice or a hook around it, which would you choose?
Where do most of your bad drives finish?

That last one is especially important and reveals much about your swing. Your driver is your straightest-faced club, so shots hit with it

FIG. 1 Your driver has less loft than your wedge, so it is harder to hit straight.

are going to curve the most. The shape of your drives exposes your swing tendencies. That comes as a big shock to most people. It isn't because the driver is bigger. Or longer. Or heavier. It's because of the face. The lack of loft causes you to hit more in the middle of the ball, which means that if the face is open or closed, your shots will have substantial curve right or left. More loft produces more backspin on your ball, which counteracts any sidespin. That's why it is relatively easy to hit a straight shot with your wedge.

The answers I get to those questions tell me how knowledgeable you are. How much you understand about what you are trying to do is important. What is the strength of your game? The weak points? What would you like to improve? It is, after all, your golf game I am trying to fix. I want you to be happy. And that usually means an improved ball-flight and better shots. If the ball flies too high, I'll bring it down; too low, I'll move it up. If every shot curves to the right or left, I'll straighten them out.

Plus, it always helps to know what you, the student, is thinking. Have you had other lessons? Who from? Different teachers teach different theories.

The bottom line, however, is that the responses I get to those questions give me somewhere to start and tell me what sort of swing faults you are likely to have. Which, of course, is the whole point of you coming to see me in the first place. Proper diagnosis is the first step toward curing any problem.

Okay, let's see you hit some shots. Watching you will give me even more clues as to how to go about fixing your faults. There's no need to feel embarrassed. Everyone has swing faults. And I mean everyone. Even my most famous pupil, Mark O'Meara, has tendencies and little mistakes he constantly has to look for in his action. And he always will, even if he did perform well enough to win two major championships and be player of the year in 1998. So, believe me, you won't be telling me anything I haven't heard many times before.

Here's what I'll be paying most attention to:

BALL-FLIGHT

All golfers have one of two tendencies. Either your shots will move predominantly from left-to-right or mostly from right-to-left. In other words, you're either a slicer or a hooker. Most people, of course, slice.

And there's more. Your shots start off straight at your target or to the right or left (see fig. 2). And you hit the ball too high, too low, or on the proper trajectory for your clubhead speed. In an ideal world, a perfectly on-plane swing will produce a gentle draw shot, the ball curving slightly from right-to-left. That is fact. Indeed, I have never heard a teacher dispute this point. Here's why.

Because you are standing to the side of the ball, the club should swing to the inside of the ball-target line in the backswing, to straight at impact, to back to the inside in the through swing. So you want to contact the inside part of the ball with the clubface closing as it comes through in order to start your little draw to the right of the target.

When I first started working with Mark O'Meara he represented the Ben Hogan Company. One day, in Mr. Hogan's office, Mark asked him what the correct flight on a perfectly struck shot should be. He told Mark exactly what I have just told you.

Mark then asked another question: "When you hit that draw should the clubface be square, closed, or slightly open but in the process of closing?"

Mr. Hogan looked at Mark for a long moment. Then he asked who had told Mark to ask that question. Mark said, "My teacher, Hank

FIG. 2 There are three possibilities with every shot: hook, slice, or straight.

Haney." "You tell him he's right," was Mr. Hogan's reply. When I heard that I knew I had asked an intelligent question and I knew I was on the right track.

Every time I give a lesson I get ball-flight results. All because I'm looking at the flight of the ball and impact. Changing one has to change the other. If you get stuck changing things that have nothing to do with the flight of the ball you get into trouble. You get no change to the ball-flight or impact and frustration is the result.

For example, what good is it saying that you swung too fast? How is swinging slower going to change impact? If the change made has no immediate effect on your shots, then the best you can say about it is that it is a building block for the future. In that regard, such a change can be worthwhile. But a change in ball-flight is what you are really after. Never lose sight of that.

IMPACT

If you're going to hit a better shot, you have to change the geometry of what is happening in your swing as club strikes ball. More questions:

Is the club coming into the ball too much from the outside or the inside?

Is the angle of the shaft as it comes into the ground too steep or too shallow?

Is the clubface open or closed?

Where is the bottom of your swing—at, behind, or too far ahead of the ball?

Have you increased or decreased the loft on the clubface?

Improvement in any or all of those angles will improve your ball-striking.

Wait a minute, I can hear you saying. What about my swing? What about my grip? What about my stance? Don't those things come before I hit the ball?

Only chronologically. If you really want to make a positive difference to any aspect of your game or swing, you have to understand what it is you are trying to achieve.

When I start an analysis of your game, I first look at the flight of the ball. Then I work back. The flight of the ball basically tells you what happened at impact. Changing what your shots are doing means first changing what happens between club and ball at impact. Your main goal is to change how the ball flies, so you have to change impact. That will lead us to the swing plane. Changing that, changes impact. But in order to change your swing plane you must change something your hands and arms and/or your body are doing. So you go (a) ball-flight, (b) impact, (c) swing plane.

Impact controls which way the golf ball goes. Any change you make to your swing has to have some influence on impact. Most golfers say they have five different swings. They may feel that way, but the reality is that if the ball-flight is the same no matter what they are feeling, they only have one impact. If you had five different swings, you'd have five different ball-flights.

All of my teaching is designed to create a better impact. To do that you have to find out what kind of impact you have to begin with. A correct impact is one where the club is coming into the ball from the inside with the clubface square to the arc of the swing.

But is that yours? Where do your shots start—left or right? Does the ball curve left or right? Does the club come into the ball on the proper angle of approach? In other words, are you digging in too much, or hitting too shallow? If the bottom of the swing is in the right place, you're not hitting either in front of the ball or behind it. Test yourself. Make a line of tees on the ground (see fig. 3). Can you hit one? Or do you tend to bottom out in front or behind the line?

If your impact is correct, it follows that you will also have the correct loft on the club, which is indicated by the trajectory on the shot. You won't add loft by breaking down your left wrist at impact, or take too much loft off the club by bending your right wrist back incorrectly. A fast-paced swing will hit the ball higher because it imparts more spin. A slower swing generally produces lower shots.

FIG. 3 Find the bottom of your swing by trying to hit a line of tees.

It comes down to this. To create a totally correct impact, you need a fundamentally correct swing. If you haven't got that, you will always be missing something at impact. Which is where your analysis has to come from.

Ask yourself: What am I trying to fix here? It isn't the speed of my swing. It isn't the role of my right elbow in the swing. It isn't my left knee. It isn't my shoulder turn. I am trying to fix my impact.

Any correction you make has to directly or indirectly affect impact. Anything else may make your swing look "prettier," but it won't really have any positive effect on the quality of your shots. So why bother?

WHAT THE CLUB IS DOING

The club is the thing that hits the ball, so what it does as it moves from address to impact and beyond is the most important aspect of your swing. I don't buy the notion that if your body moves correctly, the club is going to all of a sudden do everything right. That just doesn't ring true. I look at the body merely as something that needs to work properly in order to give your hands and arms the opportunity to do the right things. That's not to say your torso is unimportant, but there is no guarantee that making a good turn leads automatically to a good swing. There are too many other variables. What I will say is that a poor body turn leaves you with little or no chance of making a good swing.

So I don't fix a bad body motion unless doing so has a direct influence on the club. For example, if you come to me with a reverse pivot—your weight moving to your front foot on the backswing, then to your back foot on the downswing—then your body is the first thing I am going to work on. That's where I'll start, but only because it gives me a chance to improve the role of your hands and arms and the club.

SWING PLANE

In any swing the club has to move in and around your body and it has to move up and down. If you're swinging on the correct plane you've got just the right amount of in and just the right amount of up in your backswing, the club moving on an arc around your body. When the club swings on a natural arc, the face squares up more easily. Think of it as like hitting a tennis ball or clapping your hands.

That's the ideal, but there are two other possibilities. If you swing the club on too much of a straight line—too upright (see fig. 4)—coming into the ball, you're going to tend to open the clubface through impact. If you swing the club on too much of an arc—too flat (see fig. 5)—the clubface will tend to close too quickly through the hitting area.

So the swing plane determines to a great extent whether or not the clubface is going to be square coming into the ball. Or, at least, a correct swing plane gives you your best chance to get the face square. That's not to say you can't make an upright swing then flip your hands over through impact, or make a flat swing and hold the face open with

FIG. 4 Swinging on too upright a plane invariably leads to a slice.

FIG. 5 Swinging on too flat a plane usually leads to a hook.

your hands, but both are difficult to do consistently. It's hard to get everything just right on anything other than an occasional basis.

Another thing the swing plane does for you is determine where you're going to hit on the clubface. How much the club swings behind you on the backswing influences how much in front of you it swings on the downswing.

If the club comes down on too upright a plane, the clubhead will be closer to your feet than it should be. So you will tend to hit the ball off the toe of the club.

If you swing down on too flat a plane, the club will tend to swing too much out in front of you. So you will contact the ball with the heel of the club.

Lastly, the plane of your downswing determines how much ground you are going to hit. How much the club moves up influences how much it swings down. If it goes up too much, it will come down too much. Unless you do something to flatten your downswing. But if the club comes down on too upright a plane you will tend to hit the ball fat. Too flat a downswing leads to thin shots more often than not.

Compare that information with the answers you gave to my original questions. A few of your swing tendencies and what they lead to should be emerging.

NOT A TYPICAL LESSON

Most golf instruction is simply more of that "why bother?" stuff. You know the kind of thing, the kind of lesson, I mean. I bet you've had more than a few of these sessions over the years.

The first thing your "teacher" does is change your grip. Not for any particular reason, merely to fit some kind of mythical ideal he's read in a book. Besides, moving his pupil's hands on the club is the way he begins every lesson. Then he works on your aim. Then he tells you to swing slower.

Just so you know, here's why we won't be starting with those things and why they may not even come up at all.

THE GRIP

I never change anyone's grip unless the golf ball tells me to. In other words, if you are hooking and you have a strong grip—your hands turned too far to the right on the club—you need to change your grip. Same if you are slicing and have a weak grip.

But if you are, say, slicing your shots and you have a strong grip, you sure don't want to be changing the way you hold onto the club. Making your grip more neutral is only going to make your ball-flight worse. That's just simple logic.

The only other time I go straight to your grip is if it doesn't allow you to cock your wrists properly, or if your grip pressure is too soft or too tight.

AIMING

If you're like most golfers, you think you have a problem aiming. Not necessarily so. Aiming problems usually stem from the fact that every club in your bag has a different amount of loft and so creates a different amount of backspin. Backspin counteracts sidespin. If you have a curvature mistake the ball will curve a different amount with every club in your bag. That means you need a different aim for every club in the bag. Way too complicated.

So the reason you have trouble aiming is that you have trouble hitting the ball straight. How can you aim straight—indeed, why would you want to?—if you can't hit straight? But don't worry about it. Aim is way overrated; it isn't nearly as important as some people make it out to be. Once you can hit the ball straight—and when you've finished this book you will have the capability to do just that—you'll find the right aim. When you look at a golf course, the fairways are typically 40 yards wide. Greens are about 30 yards across. How good do you have to aim to hit a ball onto a fairway or a green? Not very. It's difficult to misaim by as much as 40 yards.

Alignment, however, is important. Make sure everything is coordinated—feet, knees, hips, shoulders, eyes, arms—and pointed in the same direction (see fig. 6). They must be parallel to one another and parallel to the clubface alignment. Aiming is a different issue. Aiming at a specific target isn't worth worrying about until you can hit a straight ball.

FIG. 6 At address, everything—eyes, shoulders, arms, hips, legs, and feet—should be aligned parallel to the ball-target line.

SWING SPEED

"My swing is too quick." This may be the biggest misconception ever. Think about it. If you take a fast, lousy swing and slow it down all you've got left is a slow, lousy swing. Most people swing too slow, not too fast. The minimum speed on the PGA Tour for a driver is 110 mph. Average golfers swing at about 85 mph. Yet they think they're going too fast.

The reality is that their techniques are bad and they may be swinging too hard. But too fast? No. Maybe too fast in the wrong places, but in general too slow. The correctness of a swing is much more important than the speed. Fix the things in your swing which have a direct bearing on the flight of your shots. That is all that matters.

FORGET "HOW-TO"

Such emphasis on your faults should tell you that this is not a "how-to" golf book, like so many of the others you can find on the shelves in your local bookshop. All the help and information you gather from this book will be based on how you hit the ball. You. Not some mythical being who does everything perfectly; you.

Besides, you aren't going to "how-to" it with this book. Most golfers don't how-to it even with a how-to book. They don't start at chapter one and work on everything in there, then move on to chapter two. And so on. That's not how people read golf books. If you are like every other golfer I have ever met, you are going to get in the middle somewhere, find the part you think deals with your mistake, and work on that. The one thing you won't do is start at the beginning.

This book isn't like that. We're not going to say, "Good golf starts with a good grip." Then move on to the stance and aiming "correctly" like seemingly hundreds of golf instruction books have done over the years. Unless you are a complete beginner, those volumes are of little use to you anyway.

ANALYZE—DIAGNOSE—FIX

I take the view that if you are coming to me for a lesson—which is what this book is going to be for you—you are already a golfer, you already have a golf swing, and you already have faults in that swing. That's why there are very few absolutes in these pages. This is a golf book—a golf lesson—designed to fix your faults and make you a better player, but there isn't only one way to achieve either or both. Hopefully, you'll have some fun along the way, too.

Here is how we are going to achieve all of the above. And the great thing is, everything I am going to tell you over the course of this book is all perfectly logical, if you stop to think about it. As I've said, in order to correct an error, you have to be able to analyze and diagnose exactly what it is you are doing wrong. And in order to diagnose what you are doing wrong you have to be able to understand what the clues are, so to speak, that can lead you on your way to properly analyzing your game.

That's why the answers to my list of questions are so important, along with what your swing feels like and looks like. Those responses are the routes along which you first diagnose your problems, analyze them, then fix them. Think about it. A golf swing takes only about a second and a half to complete, so you can't be telling yourself ten different things to do between address and finish. You need a simple picture in your mind of the swing you are trying to make and, most importantly, how that swing feels.

So make things easy for yourself. Start with the critical errors, the ones that are really influencing the flight of your golf ball. At any given time and any given swing you could look at your method and find many things wrong with it. But most of those faults aren't that important. Which is why your diagnosis must lead to you formulating a plan. You must have a plan. If you don't you'll be wandering around aimlessly and never get to any kind of positive result.

You don't want to be making the same mistakes I did. When I was a youngster I used to practice all the time; I was a real hard worker. And that was one of the things that led me into teaching. I had lessons growing up. They helped but I had nothing to judge them against. When I think back now and look at some of the results my students get, I realize that the teaching I received was poor. The results I produce are much more dramatic.

Twenty-odd years ago I was hearing the basic fundamentals: grip, setup, stance, posture, make a full shoulder turn, don't swing too quick, swing smooth—all the boring old clichés. And, sadly, that was how most pros taught the game to their pupils.

Even more sadly, the same basic problems still hold true today. It pains me to say this, but the average golf instructor in this country isn't that good. Not only that, there just isn't that much difference in the way most teachers teach. Until you get to the top instructors, that is. Then there's a huge difference. Which is why they are the best: they stand out from the crowd. But there isn't much between very good and poor.

HOW I EVOLVED AS A TEACHER

As I went through my golf career in college, I realized that I wanted to be a teacher. I started giving lessons at recreational centers in Tulsa, Oklahoma. Then I got lucky. I had the opportunity to work with a man named Jim Hardy. He was the person who really had the greatest influence on me in terms of my teaching. Jim had such an incredible mind for the game of golf. He took me under his wing and gave me the best start anyone could ever have in learning how to teach.

After graduating I went back to my hometown of Chicago and began teaching for John Cleland at the Exmoor Country Club. John really gave me the chance to get started. I think he felt early on that my teaching had the potential to be something special. At first, I was basically teaching what I had learned from Jim Hardy, but it was around that time I had my first experience with the John Jacobs method of teaching. Jim was teaching with the John Jacobs golf schools at the time. Jacobs had a great system for teaching. Everything was based on the flight of the golf ball. Some people thought Jacobs' method was a little bit of a Band-aid approach, but the big plus I saw was that both the teacher and the student saw immediate results.

Jacobs wasn't just a great "quick-fix" routine, however. Every pupil left with a much nicer shape to their swings, so it looked to me like they had a chance to improve over the long term, too. It was also simple. It was like, okay, these people slice so we have to do this, this, and this; these people hook, so we do that, that, and that. John Jacobs is the best teacher the game of golf has ever seen.

Let me repeat, however, that everything was based on the ball-flight. Ball-flight told John the direction he had to go with every pupil. It was a great system and one that was easily applied. Look at the ball-flight, look at the swing, and go from there. Even today, that is the basic method I use when giving a lesson.

At about the same time, 1978, I went to a Professional Golf Association (PGA) Business School. There was a section on teaching. I went along thinking that because I had worked with the John Jacobs schools I had a good knowledge of instruction. I was wrong; I was way better than that.

While I still had—and continue to have—much to learn, what I heard that day shocked me. After listening to a variety of teachers, I came away very disappointed. The quality of the instruction was really poor. Which, when you think about it, isn't that surprising. It is only recently that the PGA has introduced a certification program for teachers. Before that you had to get lucky, in that the only way to get a decent foundation in instruction was to go work for a PGA pro who happened to be a decent teacher. And, as I've said, there weren't too many of them around.

At that time the best teachers in the country worked for Jacobs and the Golf Digest Schools. Men like Jacobs, Hardy, Shelby Futch, Bob Toski, Jim Flick, Davis Love, and Peter Kostis. They were all terrific and had the added benefit of being very different personality types. Every pupil left these golf schools having benefited from at least one of those great instructors.

So what did I hear at that now long-forgotten seminar that was so bad? I heard the beginning of every golf book written to that point. You know the sort of thing. Here's your grip. Here's your stance. And here's your posture. The problem with that is it doesn't really get to the heart or the essence of teaching. When a student comes to me for a golf lesson, he presumably would like to leave hitting better shots.

I can tell you how much better your grip, setup, and swing looks until I am blue in the face, but if you came slicing and left still slicing, in your mind you haven't really improved. Which is true. If your shots aren't better, your scores won't be either. So, to me, teaching has to first relate to hitting better shots. Which leads to better scores.

Let me tell you one more thing: There is no reason why anyone coming to me for a lesson should have to get worse before they get better.

Well, almost no reason. Sometimes people do get worse for a short time. That's because golf is such a game of mistakes. If you have an even number of mistakes you can play really well. That was one of the things John Jacobs showed. He could balance out mistakes. Even if someone didn't have a perfect swing, he helped them by prescribing a little stronger grip to make up for the slice motion in the swing, or a little different ball position to make up for the bottom of the swing being in the wrong place.

TWO, FOUR, SIX, OR EIGHT

When you hit good golf shots you have an even number of mistakes. Preferably zero, but two, four, six, or eight works well, too. As long as everything matches up. The problem is that, although every golfer hits good shots occasionally, they all want to be more consistent. When you match up too many mistakes it's hard to be consistent.

If you get worse after a lesson, it's because you have ruined the balance in your swing. You used to have six mistakes; three mistakes balancing out three others. Now you have maybe three mistakes. But the compensations are gone. So for a short period you struggle. That's why you have to put the whole thing together in your mind. You have to know exactly what you're trying to fix so that you don't get things out of balance. So you don't make them worse before they get better. If one thing is changed, the compensation has to be changed, too.

For example, if you swing too upright, you will tend, as I've said, to hit into the ground too deep (see fig. 7). As a result, you will pull up, away from the ball through impact (see fig. 8a and 8b). Hitting the ground so hard shakes your hands, elbows, and shoulders, and you get tired of that whole scenario pretty quickly. So you lift up with your arms, with your posture, with your hands; you come up in some way to avoid hitting into the ground.

You have two mistakes: an upright swing and a spine angle changing to compensate for that swing. The first thing I need to do is get you swinging on a flatter plane. I do that. But you are still coming out of your posture. So you are topping the ball.

Technically, of course, at this point your swing is better. But you are hitting poorer shots. Which is not what you want or I want. So it's time to fix the postural error. Although mistakes have to be fixed in pairs, there is always an order to things. There is always a number one error and a number two.

Of course, I won't let things get to that stage. I plan for it. I know that flattening the swing will cause you to top the ball, so I let you hit off a tee at first. That way, even if you do come out of your posture a little bit, you'll still hit a decent shot. And, more importantly, you won't hit a series of "grounders" and become discouraged. In fact, it'll be just the opposite. Your ball-flight will improve immediately, just because your swing is now on a better plane. That gives you a better opportunity to square the clubface as you smack the back of the ball.

The triangle formed by the hands, arms, and shoulders should be right in front of the body.

Every part of Mark's body is square (parallel left of the target-line). Good posture—a slight bend from the hips, the arms hanging down from the shoulders.

The club, already well off the ground, swings back along the original angle of the clubshaft.

When the club is parallel to the ground it should also be parallel to the target-line.

Mark's arms stay out in front of his body as his shoulders turn.

On plane on the way to the top.

At the top the club points parallel left of the target with the left wrist, the left arm and the clubface lined up and on plane.

Mark's shoulders have turned to ninety degrees while his hips have turned only about half as much. Notice how his hands and arms have not swung past his turn. His hands are still out in front of his body.

Mark's hands and arms have lowered the club to start the downswing and the clubshaft is still on plane.

There is a lateral motion of the hips to start the downswing, the right shoulder staying back to bring the club into the ball from the inside.

The club descends through the same plane it rose through on the backswing. From here the angle of approach can be correct.

The club is again out in front of the body at this point.

The back of Mark's left hand is square to the target, with his weight well into his left side.

Mark's hips are leading his body through.

Mark's hands have released the club to a point of full extension.

Lower body is forward while the upper body stays back.

The clubshaft is still on plane—above but parallel to the original angle of the shaft.

A proper hit from the inside with full release and extension leads to a high finish.

Mark's hips and shoulders have turned through to face the target. His hands have hinged to the finish and his eyes are up to follow the ball.

Perfect balance!

FIG. 7 Too upright a swing can lead to too deep an impact.

FIG. 8 Swing too steeply for awhile and you will inevitably begin to lose your posture from address (a) to impact (b) in an effort to hit less ground.

If things go really well, I might not have to work on the spine angle problem at all. You were coming out of your posture because your swing plane was too steep. Curing the swing problem can also make the second mistake go away.

People do things wrong in golf for one of two reasons: habit or necessity. If the spine angle you have at address is different from the spine angle you have at impact because your swing is too steep, that's a necessity. If your spine angle didn't change, you'd crash into the ground and hit the ball fat, which is one of the worst shots in golf. It also hurts your body.

Then again, there are those who swing badly out of habit. For example, if our steep swinger flattens his swing plane but continues to change his spine angle, he's doing so simply because it feels "normal." He used to come out of his posture to keep from hitting the ground. Now he doesn't need to do that, but he does it anyway. All because he's used to it. But that won't continue for long. Pretty soon he'll get the idea that he doesn't have to pull up to avoid hitting the ground. Then he'll gain confidence, knowing he can stay in his posture and release the club all the way to the ground without hitting the shot fat. Then he'll be well on the way to breaking his habit.

Those are the two ways I look at a problem. People either have a mistake which necessitates another mistake, or they have one mistake which oftentimes is just a bad habit left over from a time when they did have two mistakes.

Most teachers don't put that all together. Most teachers get stuck on looking at something in a golf swing that they don't like. Sometimes it's something that they themselves are working on. I've often thought that, before every lesson, teachers should have to write down what they are working on in their own swings—then not be allowed to teach it. Teachers tend to get on kicks. They work on the left knee or the right elbow, or on something they happen to be keyed into for some period of time. Then they teach that same thing to every student. At the Masters one year I once saw a teacher prescribe the exact same move to six different touring pros. Can you imagine that every one had the same mistake at the same time? I can't.

Teachers experiment on students, too. They try new things. They try things that worked for someone else. They try anything. Now, while I have no doubt that every teacher does his or her best for each and every pupil, the problem is that most teachers have trouble formulating a plan.

THE PLAN

To fix a problem, you must have a plan. You have to figure out what it is that you are trying to fix. There are two ways to go. You can either fix your ball-flight, or you can develop your swing. Swing development means trying to swing a certain way. You have a picture of the swing you want in your mind and you work toward that goal. The idea, of course, is that if you make a perfect swing you'll hit a perfect shot.

Now, theoretically there is a perfect swing, but I don't think anybody has one. Certainly, I've never seen one and I'm not sure it is attainable. But that doesn't seem to stop the "swing model" guys. They're stuck on the idea that the better your swing is, the better you'll hit the ball. But, as I've already pointed out, that isn't necessarily so.

The other approach is, to me, much simpler. It's like, okay, you're slicing; this is what causes you to slice and this is what we need to do to fix your slice. And that is what helps you to make a plan. You need to blend the two approaches.

Early in my career I focused almost exclusively on error correction. Which can shortchange some pupils. The person who really wants to get better or develop his game or wants to grow as a player can get left out. The short-term approach isn't for him.

So I've tried to blend the two together. Always achieving short-term results, but never losing sight of the fact that every player also wants to have long-term progress. In order to do that you have to have a good plan. A good start is encouraging, but you also have to know where you are headed.

To me, that good start is a better ball-flight. Nowadays, so much of teaching is done with video, comparing a student's swing with that of a tour pro. Instructors spend hours showing students how much better they look. But there's a downside. When someone leaves that teacher, gets out on the course, and doesn't hit the ball better, he rarely falls back on his improved appearance while hitting poor shots. Instead, he worries over the fact that he is still hitting the ball badly.

That's why focusing on the ball-flight works. It gives you hope and encouragement and confidence in me, the teacher. So I start with some sort of ball-flight error correction. That's the most important thing. A good plan starts with, "What is my ball doing?" Keep going back to your original questions.

Then, "What is my ball-flight and what is my golf club doing wrong during the swing to cause the golf ball to fly a certain way?"

"What are the body, hands, and arms doing to make the golf club do something wrong?"

"What do I need the club to do better?"

"What do I need my body, hands, and arms to do to make my club do something better?"

I work from there, blending the two, long term and short term, together. That way, I don't lose anyone. The dedicated student is happy and so is the guy who just wants to stop slicing. I like to think my teaching offers something for everyone.

SWING PLANE

I make no apologies for returning to this subject so soon. But the swing plane is the basis for my teaching—and will be for your learning.

The plane of the swing is a big area of confusion for most golfers. Everyone has a certain plane that they should swing on. It isn't the same for everyone, but there is a plane for everyone. Everyone is different. We all have different heights, different length arms, different distances we stand from the ball, different postures; lots of variables. All those factors affect your swing plane.

There are three possibilities when it comes to swing plane. You are either on the correct plane, above it (too upright), or below it (too flat). It's that simple. As a result, every golfer's strength tends to be with either their longer clubs or their shorter clubs. If your swing is on the steep side, you'll typically be better with your shorter irons (see fig. 9a). With a wood or long iron you'll be standing further from the ball (see fig. 9b), which means your swing will naturally be flatter. So, if your swing is too upright, your fault will show up more.

As you'd expect, the opposite is also true. If you err on the flat side of perfect, you'll likely be better with woods and struggle with your short irons.

So everyone falls into one of two categories. There aren't many possibilities. Most students don't analyze their games enough. When I ask people where their ball goes, the most common answer is, "Everywhere." Well, that doesn't tell us anything. If you sit and analyze where most of your shots go, there will always be a pattern. But most people don't think about it.

FIG. 9 With a short iron in your hands (a), you will naturally stand closer to the ball than you would with a long iron (b).

A GAME OF MISTAKES

When I explain to a student that golf is a game of mistakes, I tell them that for the next fifteen minutes they might hit some really bad shots because they are caught in between old and new. But that doesn't mean to say you should give up trying to do the right things in your swing. Persevere through the bad times. Show some commitment. Even the best players in the world struggle with their games.

Don't judge how you are doing by how anyone else does. Golf is an individual game. So do your own thing. Work at your pace and get better at your pace. You can't worry about what everyone else is doing. That applies just as much when you are struggling. Everyone struggles sometimes. It's hard to change but you can do it.

I remember when I started working with Mark O'Meara in 1982. He did better right away but then in '83 he had times when he struggled. At one point he missed four cuts in a row and came to see me in Pinehurst. I thought that this was the crossroads for him. He could either give up on his plan, or he could dig in and keep trying. Which is what he did. Mark showed what he was made of. He kept going and cleared the hurdle.

Everyone has doubts when taking a lesson. Is this going to work for me? Am I going to be able to do it? Sometimes they doubt themselves; sometimes they doubt the teacher. That can lead to a different teacher, a different swing thought, and, ultimately, confusion.

Stick with what you know. Understand your golf swing. Know what causes the ball to fly in different directions. Understand why your ball doesn't. Then have a plan to fix it.

AND LET'S BE POSITIVE!

When people come for lessons I have to motivate them to do better. Every golfer I've ever seen could do better. And I've never had a lesson I would label a failure. I've never had a student fail. And I don't anticipate you will either.

Analyze what your golf ball does. Make a plan to fix your faults. Work on it and you'll get better. It takes time, it takes practice, and most of all it takes patience. Golf is a very difficult game. The best players in the world get a lot of help with their games, so why shouldn't you. There is nothing wrong with slow, steady improvement. You just have to be very patient with yourself and practice as much as you can. That doesn't mean four hours a day every day; you just have to apply yourself. Think good thoughts and increase your understanding of what you are trying to do. Know your goal.

Most golfers I see at driving ranges aren't practicing; they're merely exercising. They really don't have an idea of what they are doing wrong—or right. They don't have a plan for fixing anything. They're just out there searching for the "secret." Well, the secret is that there isn't a secret. Or, at least, no easy option. Ben Hogan once said that the secret is in the dirt. In other words, you have to practice.

Now, you can argue that you are simply out there to have fun hitting some balls. And that's fair enough. But you can have even more fun hitting the ball better. There's a limit to how much fun you can have slicing every shot. Take my word for it.

Besides, golf is really error correction. That's why this book is set up the way it is. You have already played golf. You already have a certain pattern to your game. Now you need to correct what it is you are doing wrong. That's how you get better. Let's get to it and before long your game will be coming on.

2

Fit Your Clubs to Your Game

This happens all the time. I watch a new student hit only a few shots, then I ask what he is working on in terms of his swing. I get all kinds of answers.

"Shifting my weight."
"I'm trying not to sway."
"Keeping my head still."
"Not coming over the top."

Sadly, all of those replies miss the point. If any or all of them sound familiar, you have fallen into an all-too common trap. Instead of working on making your technique better, you are stuck trying to fix the results of your current bad swing. In other words, you are working on the results of something you are doing wrong, rather than the root cause of your swing problem.

Again, that is the essence of my teaching—finding the real reason why a problem is happening, fixing it, then letting that fix change the effect. For instance, most people who come "over the top" at the start of the downswing move the club too much to the inside early in the backswing. In turn, that fault typically stems from pushing the hands too far forward at address.

Most people see something that is wrong, but don't see what caused it. Which is why golf is such a hard game. And why you have to be good at diagnosing.

Before we start to work on your swing faults, I look for ways to fix problems without any effort from you. Everyone is always up for that.

While I watch those first few shots of yours, I'm looking at your ball-flight and swing shape. But I'm also taking note of the clubs you are using. They may or may not be allowing you the opportunity to make a good swing. In fact, to be honest, there is almost always a problem. In my experience nine out of ten golfers would be better served using different equipment. You're not giving yourself a chance to make good swings and hit good shots if your clubs are not fitted to your body type and swing.

Let's say you are 6'4". If your clubs are standard length and lie (the angle at which the shaft extends from the head), you don't have a chance to make good contact with the ball. Not consistently anyway. It won't happen because your clubs won't let you do it. In this case they will be both too short and too flat. What will happen is that your swing will compensate for your inappropriate equipment. End result? An equally inappropriate swing.

WHERE TO LOOK FOR PROBLEMS

A good worker never blames his tools, they say, but that isn't the case in golf. Your clubs need to be specific to your needs. Here's what to look for:

Shaft Length

Shafts that are short will cause you to bend over too much and stand too close to the ball. Shafts that are long will force you to stand too tall and too far from the ball. Either way, the plane of your swing is going to be affected.

Lie

A club that sits too upright means your hands will be too high at address. A club that sits too flat leads to your hands being too low at address. Again, your swing will have to compensate for either.

Grip Circumference

If a grip is thick or thin, the ability of your hands to work properly during the swing will be affected. That's important. Your hands are your only points of contact with the club, which is what makes contact with the ball.

Shaft Flex

A shaft that is stiff for your swing will cost you distance. A shaft that is "whippy" will tend to make you less accurate than you could be.

Driver Loft

In a misguided attempt to hit lower shots and/or gain yardage, most golfers use a driver that doesn't have enough loft. More loft means less sidespin which means greater accuracy. And, invariably, doesn't cost you much in the way of distance.

Set Makeup

Are you making the most of the fourteen clubs that the rules of golf allow you?

There are many different factors. But the common factor is that any mistake in your clubs has to match up with a mistake in your setup and/or your swing. Let's look at each in turn.

LENGTH AND LIE

Clubs have always been made for the average height individual, but over the years this has changed. For example, the center on the basketball team used to be 6½ feet tall. Nowadays that's the guard's height. So everyone is getting taller and clubs, in turn, are getting longer. When I was growing up in the mid-sixties a normal 2-iron was 38½ inches long. Now it is 39¼.

So, if you are not average height, chances are your clubs don't fit you. The most important aspects of any club are the shaft length and the lie. They work in conjunction. Lie angle affects how far the butt end of the club is up off the ground. If you add an inch to the length of a club you don't really get the full inch because the shaft rises at an angle.

If you want to make your clubs effectively longer, you need to make them more upright, too. Always go in increments. A little at a time. For every degree more upright a club is, you effectively make it about ³/₈ of an inch longer.

That's why, if your height, posture, and length of arms make me think you need longer clubs, I don't only recommend you lengthen the shafts. You need to make them more upright, too. Moving away from the ball isn't necessarily going to help your swing. Every golfer needs a good posture (more on that later), the hands hanging down beneath the shoulders, with the bend forward from the hips around twenty degrees (see fig. 10). Nice and comfortable.

FIG. 10 At address, create an angle of about twenty degrees between your upper and lower body.

*Fit Your Clubs to
Your Game*

FIG. 11 The distance
from your knuckles to the
ground is key when
determining the length of
your clubs.

HOW LONG?

The length of your back, arms, and legs are all factors in how long your clubs should be. But the most important aspect is the distance between your knuckles and the floor when your arms are hanging by your sides (see fig. 11). Fingertips to floor is no good because you might have unusually large hands. Small or big hands and/or short or long fingers can skew the measurement. Besides, either or both indicates you need a different grip size, not shorter or longer clubs.

Knuckle to Ground (length in inches)	Length of 5-iron
22	31
23	32
24	33
25	34
26	35
26–27$\frac{1}{4}$	36$\frac{1}{4}$
27$\frac{1}{4}$–28$\frac{1}{2}$	36$\frac{3}{4}$
28$\frac{1}{2}$–29$\frac{3}{4}$	37$\frac{1}{4}$
29$\frac{3}{4}$–31	37$\frac{3}{4}$ (standard length)
31–33$\frac{1}{2}$	38$\frac{1}{4}$
33$\frac{1}{2}$–34$\frac{3}{4}$	38$\frac{3}{4}$
34$\frac{3}{4}$–36	39$\frac{1}{4}$
36–37$\frac{1}{2}$	39$\frac{3}{4}$

Palm Size	Finger	Grip Size
3$\frac{1}{4}$–3$\frac{1}{2}$	2$\frac{3}{8}$–2$\frac{1}{2}$	–$\frac{1}{32}$
3$\frac{1}{2}$–3$\frac{3}{4}$	2$\frac{5}{8}$–2$\frac{3}{4}$	–$\frac{1}{64}$
3$\frac{3}{4}$–4	2$\frac{7}{8}$–3	standard
4–4$\frac{1}{4}$	3–3$\frac{1}{4}$	+$\frac{1}{64}$
4$\frac{1}{4}$–4$\frac{1}{2}$	3$\frac{3}{8}$–3$\frac{1}{2}$	+$\frac{1}{32}$
4$\frac{1}{2}$–4$\frac{3}{4}$	3$\frac{5}{8}$–3$\frac{3}{4}$	+$\frac{3}{64}$
4$\frac{3}{4}$–5	3$\frac{7}{8}$–4	+$\frac{1}{16}$

NOTE: These measurements are only guidelines. Other factors like skill level and physical limitations must be considered for proper fitting of golf clubs.

WHAT TO LOOK FOR

The first indication that something needs to be done about the length of your clubs is a faulty posture (which we will cover in chapter 4). Lie and length influence your posture. And your posture influences the plane of your swing and your ability to pivot your body correctly. So it follows that the lie of the club and the way that the clubface hits the ground influences the way the ball takes off and flies.

As I watch a player I always ask myself if he could sole the club properly on the ground if he did have the correct body angles. Sometimes posture is bad because the player is trying to sole the club but can't because his clubs don't fit him.

The shape and depth of your divots can also tell you a great deal about how well-suited you are to the clubs in your bag. For example, if you are making "toe deep" divots, then the lie of your clubs is too flat. If they are "heel deep"—which is rare—your clubs are too upright.

Most times, however, the divots are toe deep. That being the case, there are three possibilities. Either you are too tall, or your arms are too short, or your swing is too upright. While there isn't much you can do—barring surgery—about the first two, you have a choice with the third. You can work on flattening your action (difficult) or simply make your clubs more upright (easy). I recommend a combination of the two.

You can change your ball-flight dramatically just by changing the lie of your clubs. The flatter the lie, the more you will hit the ball to the right; more upright and the ball will go left. The differences can be quite dramatic. If you take a 5-iron that is two degrees upright and hit the ball, say, 180 yards, then take another 5-iron, this one two degrees flat, and hit it 180 yards also, there could be as much as 20 yards difference left and right between the two balls.

Of course, that illustration wouldn't hold true for long; only one or two swings. You'd soon start compensating. And that's where inconsistency comes in. One compensation leads to another and another.

So never say just "lengthen the club." It has to be "lengthen and adjust the lie." If you need longer clubs, start with one degree upright and maybe a quarter inch longer. Then another degree and another quarter inch. And so on. You never want to have a set an inch longer that isn't two or three degrees upright. The same thing when you go shorter. I never want to see clubs more than two degrees flat, no matter how short the person is. If the club gets excessively flat, it forces you to swing on too flat a plane and it gets difficult to make solid ball-turf contact. Your club is just too close to the ground for too long a period of time if you develop a swing to match clubs that are more than two degrees flat.

Where you might go as much as four degrees upright, you never go more than two degrees flat. If you need a flatter club it's better to go shorter. Problem is, when you make a club shorter, it can cost some clubhead speed. The arc of the swing gets shorter and you can't swing the club as fast. It is almost always better to have clubs a little long and/or upright as opposed to short and/or flat.

CAVITY BACK OR BLADE?

Cavity backs distribute the weight around the heel and the toe and up and down on the club. There is no reason not to play these clubs. Some people say they like blades because they give them more feedback when they miss it. That makes no sense to me. The ball will give you plenty of feedback. You want better misses, not to tell when you've got a miss.

Today's clubs are just better designed. They give you a lot of help. You can hit the ball all over the clubface and get away with it. You can still get your shots airborne and get good distance. As for blades—even tour pros don't use them nowadays. Or at least a very low percentage of them do. If you are not using cavity-back clubs you are not using the equipment that will be the most help to you (see fig. 12).

Forged clubs and blades are easier to hit for certain shots—in the wind they keep the ball down because there isn't as much weight in the bottom of the club. And you can curve the ball easier. But those are situations geared toward better players.

SHAFT FLEX

If another club goes further than yours, check both the lofts and the length and flex of the shafts. How far you hit the ball and how fast you swing determines what shaft flex is best for you. For most amateurs that means a shaft that has a regular flex. The average golfer I

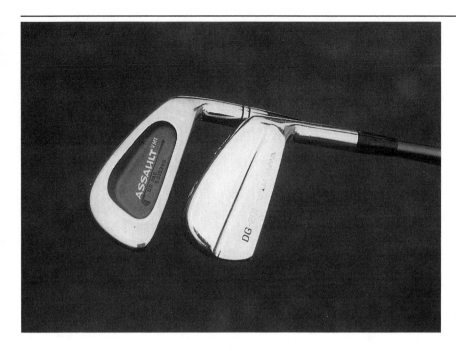

FIG. 12 Cavity-back irons
(left) will help your game
more than blades (right).

see on the range swings a driver at about 85 mph. That's a long way behind the professionals. The minimum swing speed on the PGA Tour is around 110 mph. Tiger Woods and John Daly are up at about 140 mph. That's a huge difference.

There are two factors in determining the shaft flex best for you: clubhead speed and tempo.

Someone with a slow, smooth swing—Fred Couples, John Daly—and great speed through impact doesn't need as stiff a shaft as someone with a fast action—Nick Price, Lanny Wadkins. Nick and Lanny have very stiff shafts in their clubs. Because they change direction from backswing to downswing so quickly, their shafts tend to "lag." So they need stiffness.

Find yourself in the following categories:

Slow and easy swing—regular shaft
Slow clubhead speed, quick tempo—regular-stiff shaft
Fast clubhead speed—stiff shaft
Fast clubhead speed, quick tempo—extra-stiff shaft

In general, your clubhead speed can be guessed at from your distance. And you'll already know if you have fast or slow tempo. The slower your tempo, the weaker the shaft. A faster tempo needs a stiffer shaft.

Shaft flex also affects curvature and ball-flight. A soft shaft is best if you are looking for more distance. Stiffer shafts tend to help your accuracy. So, if you are accurate but short, get softer shafts.

GRIP SIZE

These days there are many different types of grips for you to choose from. Some are better in cold weather; some in hot weather.

I find cord grips perform better in hot weather but they are hard on your hands.

Softer grips give you a firmer hold in cold weather, but they are often difficult to hold on to in sweaty summer conditions. There are no rules. Go with what you feel is most comfortable/practical for you.

Grip size is also important because it affects how your hands work in the swing. The thicker the grip, the less you will tend to use your hands. Which can lead to sliced shots.

And the opposite is true. A thinner grip will encourage hand action through impact and could lead to more hook. Once again, look at your ball-flight for clues. If you have big hands but you slice the ball, you might want bigger grips, but not too big. Grips that are big will make it hard to fix your slice.

Alternatively, if you have small hands, then you might need a smaller grip. But if you already hook the ball, take care. If the grip is thin, your hook will be hard to get rid of.

DRIVER LOFT

This is very important. Most people have drivers with shafts that are too stiff and faces with not enough loft.

That fact is especially true of slicers, the single biggest subset of golfers. People who slice tend to hit the ball high. For two reasons. One, the clubface is open at impact. And two, the clubhead is coming into the ball at too steep an angle.

So what do most slicers do? They buy a straighter-faced club in a misguided attempt to hit lower shots. A straighter face will only cause more and bigger slices. More loft means more backspin, which counteracts sidespin. So if you think that less loft means more distance, think again. What a seven-degree driver will give you is more slice or hook, not more yardage.

The trouble is, it's hard to find the right loft. There is no single answer for you, me, or anyone else. Because every club manufacturer is different. The way the weight is distributed in clubs might mean you need ten degrees in one, eight degrees in another. But the ten-degree club will always give you straighter shots. Ideally, you need to get the club with the most loft that still produces the optimum trajectory for you.

If you don't have enough loft, your shots will curve more. So you will tend to swing in the opposite direction to compensate. It's always better to have a little more loft, especially on your driver. Think about it. If you're like everyone I know, you tend to hit your 3-wood and 5-wood straighter than your driver. The increased loft is the reason why.

SET MAKEUP

Now we'll move on to the fourteen clubs you should have in your bag. The changes in this area over the last five years have been remarkable.

The Third Wedge

Beware of the club manufacturer's favorite trick. In an effort to make you think you are hitting the ball longer, they reduce the loft on your clubs. For example, a 6-iron today is about four degrees stronger than thirty years ago. That's a whole club difference and the reason why you have a big gap between the pitching wedge and the sand wedge at the end of your set. For the pitching wedge to work as it was originally designed, it needs at least fifty-two degrees loft. Nowadays some have forty-seven degrees. That's a big gap compared with the normal four-degree progression. And why every manufacturer now sells a "gap" wedge.

The evolution of the gap wedge was inevitable. As soon as one club maker bent their clubs stronger, everyone followed suit. And as soon as one club was strengthened they all had to be. It is, after all, better to have a gap at the end of the set rather than in the middle somewhere. A pitching wedge is the easiest club with which to hit a less than full shot. And even if you can't develop that shot you can always get a gap wedge.

Not long after the third wedge became acceptable, along came the lob wedge, one with as much as sixty-two degrees of loft. It became popular because people have a hard time getting the ball in the air and stopping it quickly. Suddenly that was much easier.

Carrying three wedges does give you other benefits (see fig. 13).

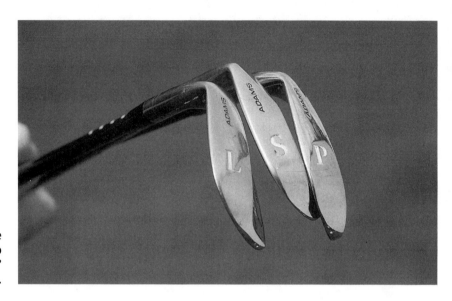

FIG. 13 Carrying three wedges means having to hit fewer "in-between" shots.

Because you have to hit fewer half and three-quarter shots, gauging distance is easier. More often than not you can go ahead and make a full swing. Especially if you are smart about laying up to specific yardages. The top pros all do that. They want to hit a full shot into the green, not some fiddling little half shot.

That's why knowing your distances is really important. Years ago Tom Kite—one of the best wedge players in the game—had his father out on the range with a walkie-talkie. He would tell Tom where each ball landed, which gave him the feedback he needed to judge how far to hit each shot. He had a feel for how hard to swing each time.

As well as following Tom's lead, you need to know what to use from 150 yards. Then there is about an 8–10 yard difference with each club.

Fairway Woods

Here's something that may shock you. If you are like most golfers, you should have at least four, maybe five, fairway woods in your bag

FIG. 14 Most golfers should carry five fairway woods; long irons are just too hard to hit.

(see fig. 14). Forget your long irons; they are just too hard to hit consistently well.

Follow the lead of the Senior Tour players and LPGA pros. They are a little bit shorter than the big guns on the PGA Tour. Those guys are so strong and powerful they only need a couple of woods in their bags. Only on special occasions—at Augusta during the Masters, for instance—would you see some of them using a 4- or 5-wood.

Seniors and women pros, although they hit the ball a long way, are more comparable to you. They use more fairway woods. Annika Sorenstam, the best woman player in the world over the last few years, has nothing longer than a 5-iron in her bag. She uses five fairway woods.

Fairway woods are easier to hit because the bottom of the club is designed with some forgiveness in mind. They are a bit like sand wedges. If you have a decent lie you can hit a sand wedge behind the ball a little and still hit a semi-decent shot. The club "skids" into the ball and builds in some margin for error.

Fairway woods are the same way. They are designed to glide or skid across the turf. And they have a lower center of gravity, which helps you get the ball up in the air. All of which makes them easier to hit. Most people have all kinds of trouble getting the bottom of their swing in the right place. So they have trouble hitting the ball and the turf at the same time. But a fairway wood allows you to hit a little behind the ball and still get away with it. In contrast, with a long iron in your hands you have to be precise. You have to hit right on the ball.

If you're not capable of hitting a drive 275 yards, you shouldn't be using a 1-iron. If you can't hit a drive 260 yards, you shouldn't have a 2-iron in your bag. If you can't drive it 245 yards, you shouldn't use a 3-iron. If you can't hit a drive 230 yards, you shouldn't carry a 4-iron. That is a pretty good rule of thumb. Eliminate irons as you go.

A fairway wood will also produce a better trajectory. The more loft you have, the more backspin you get, which means less sidespin, and the straighter you will hit the ball. More consistent. More solid. Straighter. All in all, a pretty good combination.

If you don't swing fast enough, you can't hit long irons. To hit long irons well you need a lot of clubhead speed and you have to be very precise at the bottom of the swing. Not to mention they're harder to hit straight. That's three strikes. So they're out.

Putter

Personal preference plays a big role here. The length of your putter and the lie of your putter are determined by the way you set up to the ball. The more you bend over, the better you will tend to be on short putts, not so good on long putts. Standing up, farther from your work, gives you a better view of the line on long putts, as well as a better feel for distance.

But those are generalities. Nowhere in golf is there more margin for error than in putting. Much of the time you should simply do what you feel comfortable doing.

What I will say is that your style should match your putter. There are many different types of putters. Heel-and-toe–weighted putters. Heel-shafted putters. Center-shafted putters.

If you are like Ben Crenshaw in that you like to feel the putter swinging open to closed, you will be best served by a heel-shafted putter (see figs. 15a and 15b).

If you try to keep the face square like Tom Watson, get a center-shafted putter (see figs. 16 and 16a).

Be aware that all putters have loft; somewhere between three and

 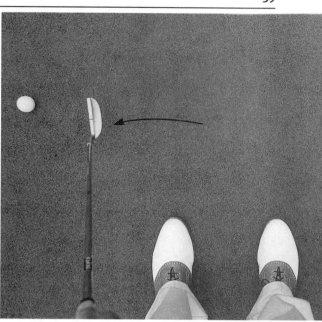

FIG. 15 A heel-shafted putter naturally creates an in-to-square-to-inside stroke shape.

FIG. 16 If you like to make a straight-back–straight-through stroke, use a center-shafted putter.

seven degrees. The more loft you have, the more the ball rolls on top of the grass. On real shaggy greens you want a more lofted club; on fast greens less loft.

But again, it depends on your style. If you like to have your hands ahead of the ball at address, you might want a putter with more loft. If your hands are more even with the ball, you'll need less loft on your putter.

3

Your Swing Plane
The Foundation

Swinging on the correct plane is the most difficult thing in golf because it is the most important thing. In fact, the swing plane isn't just the most important thing, it is the only thing.

Now, that's a pretty powerful statement when you consider that golf is ultimately supposed to be about posting the lowest score you can. But you can't do that consistently if you can't hit at least semi-decent shots.

Which is where the swing plane comes in. Let me explain.

In golf, you don't hit the ball. The way you stand to a shot doesn't hit the ball. The way you hold the club doesn't hit the ball. Your swing doesn't even hit the ball. No, only one thing hits the ball: the golf club. And the only things influencing that collision and the flight of the resulting shot are the angles on which the club is swinging into the ball. Specifically, the angle of the clubface and the angle of the shaft. So, to my mind, the swing plane is everything in that it is the one thing that has a direct bearing on the way in which club meets ball and therefore how the ball flies.

Look at it this way. If you don't change something that the club is doing, then you are not going to change the flight of the ball. Everything you do in your swing, in terms of a correction, is all to influence the plane of the swing one way or the other. If you do that, you influence the flight of the ball.

Of course, you don't swing every club on the same plane. As the club in your hand changes, so does the plane of your swing. The longer the clubshaft gets, the further you have to stand from the ball, so the flatter your plane will be. For example, if you have a wedge in your hands, you want a little more of a descending blow so you will automatically stand closer to the ball and swing on a more upright plane than you would with a 5-iron. But your thoughts and your feelings don't change. The length and lie of the club make any changes for you.

So, for me, this is the most important chapter in this book. The swing plane is the cornerstone of my teaching and, it must be said, perhaps the most misunderstood aspect of the golf swing. It has been explained many times in print, most notably and memorably by Ben Hogan in his book, *The Modern Fundamentals of Golf,* but, I don't believe it has ever been explained correctly. Hence all the confusion.

LET ME EXPLAIN

Everything you do in your golf swing has one basic aim—sending the ball to the target. Easier said than done, of course. Achieving such a goal on a consistent basis requires that you get a few things right.

A straight, solidly hit shot results when the golf club moves along the proper path, when the angle of the clubhead's approach into the impact area is correct and when the clubface is square, or squaring, as it contacts the ball. Thus, the key to any golf swing is the plane on which the club moves from address to impact. In reality, it is the only thing that matters.

As with so many other aspects of golf, there are three possibilities when it comes to swing plane. Your club is either on plane, too upright (above the plane), or too flat (below the plane). As I said in the introduction to this book, whatever your tendency, the swing plane, to a great extent, determines how much ground you are going to hit, where on the clubface you're going to hit the ball, and whether or not you are swinging on the proper arc, one which will allow the clubface to contact the ball squarely.

Every golfer has their own swing plane. Everyone is built differently and has different length arms, heights, setups—so each person has a swing plane unique to them.

WHAT DETERMINES SWING PLANE

The perfect plane for you is largely determined by your posture at address, the length of your arms, your height, and what percentage of that height is made up by your back versus your legs.

Having said that, swing planes of short and tall individuals are usually not that much different. They do vary some, but the real key is that you swing on your swing plane. The plane of someone else's swing is of no concern to you. In other words, everyone has a swing plane but there is no one swing plane for everyone. In general, tall people stand closer to the ball and have more upright swing planes. Those who are shorter tend to stand further from the ball and have flatter swing planes. Look at, say, Jeff Sluman and Nick Faldo and you'll see what I mean.

The swing plane is nothing new. As I said, it was the basis for Ben Hogan's *Modern Fundamentals*. In fact, in order to explain his swing plane philosophy, he created what may be the most famous and enduring image in golf instruction—the pane of glass angled through his shoulders and down to the ground. Hogan's theory was that you should swing the club below and parallel to the glass from address to the end of your follow-through. And that is how countless golfers have tried to swing on plane ever since.

Hogan produced a great image, but unfortunately he was wrong in this assertion. There is more than one plane in the perfect golf swing, but only one plane angle.

THE PLANE ANGLE

The plane of your swing is dictated by the angle at which the club-shaft lies at address, provided your clubs are fit correctly (see fig. 17). Ideally, you want to reproduce that angle at impact. That would be perfection. And the best, easiest, and most repeatable way to achieve that—as you'd expect—is to swing the club on the plane angle from start to finish.

Notice I'm saying that the club swings on the same plane angle, not the same plane. If you remember nothing else from this chapter, take that sentence home with you. The most important thing to understand about the swing plane and swinging on plane is that although

FIG. 17 Your plane angle is the angle of your clubshaft at address.

there is one plane angle—the angle at which you set the clubshaft at address—the club must travel through more than one plane throughout the swing.

At first glance that can seem confusing. But it isn't. Here's how it works. The club starts back along the original angle of the shaft (see fig. 18). You swing back along that plane. Then the club swings up and is above but parallel to the original angle of the shaft (see fig. 19). So it is passing through different planes.

FIG. 18 Swing the club back along your plane angle.

FIG. 19 Later in the backswing the club is above but parallel to the original plane angle.

CONGRUENT ANGLES/DIFFERENT PLANES

As you move the golf club back it consistently goes up and in, the plane of your swing constantly changing as it does so. What doesn't change is the relationship between all of those planes and the original angle of the clubshaft at address. They are always parallel.

Then, as you swing down, the club passes through those same planes on the way back to the ball (see fig. 20), all the while maintaining that parallel relationship.

FIG. 20 Swing the club down on the same plane angles as the backswing.

It's up through the planes on the backswing, down through the same planes on the downswing, and up again on the same planes on the follow-through. Achieve that and the angle of the clubshaft at impact will be the same as it was at address (see fig. 21). That is the perfect swing, one which should produce a little draw. Unfortunately, most people don't follow that path or produce that ball-flight. Most golfers have a bunch of different loops in their swings and a seemingly infinite number of different shots.

Those parallel angles are called congruent angles. In other words, they are numerically the same angle but have different points of ori-

FIG. 21 At impact the shaft should be back on your original plane angle.

gin as the club moves back and through. Therefore, the clubshaft does not always point to the target-line at all stages of the swing, as some teachers have argued in the past.

As for Hogan's pane of glass, Ben's idea is doomed from the start. Because your arms have a slight droop in them as they hang down at address, you never actually swing the club on the plane established by this imaginary pane of glass. It would be physically impossible. So don't try it. You'll hurt yourself and your game.

TWO WRONGS AND A RIGHT

Okay, so where are we? In the past the swing plane has been described in two ways. There's Hogan's way, which as we've seen is wrong.

The other way is popular among some teachers. They contend that, to be on plane, the club should either be pointing to the target-line or be parallel to that line (see fig. 22). Wrong again. If your clubshaft were to do that, your original plane angle would have to be consistently changing as your arms got higher in order to keep the clubshaft pointing at the target-line. For example, when your left arm is horizontal on the backswing, the club should be parallel to the original angle but above it. If you stayed on the original plane that would be incorrect as you would be swinging around your waist, far underneath the correct plane.

Instead, think of it this way. The higher the club gets in the swing, the more it should point above and outside the target line. Again, that's what a congruent angle is. It is parallel to but above the original angle established at address.

OFF PLANE/ON PLANE

When I say that you are swinging off plane, I mean that at some point in your swing the club is not parallel to the angle you established at address. There are two possibilities. Either the club steepens relative to the original angle of the shaft, or it flattens relative to the original angle of the shaft.

A straight-line golf swing, one which is excessively upright or

No

FIG. 22 Some people think the club should point at the target-line.

steep, produces an opening effect on the clubface and, generally, sliced shots. On the other hand, an overly flat swing creates a closing effect in the clubface and hooked shots.

An on-plane swing, in contrast, produces the proper squaring effect in the clubface through impact. That doesn't guarantee the clubface will be square as it strikes the ball, but it certainly gives you your best chance.

Notice I say "best chance." There is no guarantee. There is always the issue of timing the release. It is still possible to leave the face open by being late with the hit, or closed by hitting too early. But swinging on the correct plane does promote a natural squaring motion.

That aside, everyone who hits great shots returns the golf club to its proper plane at impact. Or they compensate for a slight change in the plane. If your swing was upright and tended to leave the face open at impact you would have to compensate somehow. Maybe by flipping your hands through impact. Or by employing a "strong" grip, your hands turned to the right on the club. Either would work, although it is harder to be consistent.

The more you get off the plane, the harder it is to square the face and the more you have to compensate. For example, come into impact too flat and you will tend to hook. So you will have to rotate your body really fast or block the release of your hands to keep the clubface from closing too rapidly.

Another factor to consider: When you swing the club on the correct plane you will hit the correct amount of ground. Ideally, your club will lightly brush the ground as it strikes the ball. An upright swing, whether in the downswing or both the backswing and downswing, will tend to hit too much ground. A flat swing means the club probably won't hit enough ground or will at least tend to bottom out behind the ball. If the club swings up the correct amount in the backswing it has its best chance to swing down the correct amount in the downswing. That gives you your best opportunity to make solid ball–turf contact.

Your swing plane also determines where you will hit the ball on the clubface. If you swing the club on the correct plane, it swings behind you the correct amount. Which allows you to swing it out in front of you the correct amount. So you hit the ball in the center of the face.

An upright swing won't swing the club around enough on the backswing. So it follows that it won't swing the club out in front enough on the downswing. Then you hit the ball off the toe of the club. If that happens to you on a consistent basis, you are either standing too far from the ball or your swing is too upright.

There is another side to the coin, of course. A flat swing has too much "around" and not enough "up." Which puts the club too far behind you on the backswing, then too far in front of you in the through swing. So you will tend to hit the ball off the heel of the club.

That's typical in golf. Things always fall into one of three categories. You hit the ball too high, too low, or just right. You hit the ball to the left, to the right, or straight. You hit in the heel, off the toe, or off the middle of the face. You hit too much ground, too little, or just enough. You are either too upright, too flat, or on plane.

THE BACKSWING

I've had pupils ask me why they should care about the plane of the backswing. Their reasoning is simple. You don't hit the ball with your backswing, so why does it matter? Isn't the downswing plane far more important?

Then they throw names like Bruce Lietzke and Jim Furyk at me. Right from address, Lietzke moves the club way to the inside on an exaggeratedly flat plane. Then he loops the club down outside his backswing on the way down. Furyk does just the opposite; his loop goes out, then in. Yet both men hit a high percentage of fairways and greens and both are very good players.

I admire both of their games. But not everyone is born with the talent of Lietzke or practices as much as Furyk. In truth, they make things more difficult for themselves, a fact they counter by having hit hundreds of thousands of balls in their lifetimes. If you don't have their talent and/or the time to hit all those balls it will be very difficult for you to make a consistent loop. The more consistent—and easier—way to swing is on plane the whole time.

I'm not saying that swinging on plane throughout is the only way to do it, of course. Some of the most accurate hitters looped it out, then in. Calvin Peete did and he was one of the straightest drivers in the history of the game. Lee Trevino, too, and Lee is one of the best ball-strikers of all time.

But they are hardly role models when it comes to teaching a model swing. It's simple really. A consistent backswing plane gives you the best chance to make a consistent downswing. The closer you get to swinging the club on the correct plane from address to impact, the more chance you have to be consistent. The more you vary from the plane on the backswing, the more corrections you have to make on the downswing to come up with a good impact.

FIND THE PROBLEM

When you look at the plane of your swing, start from address. Provided the club is set down correctly at address, check to see where it first moves off plane. You can do this in a mirror or even just by thinking about it. Once you have a picture of a perfect on-plane swing in your mind, it's easy to sense where your club is too flat or too upright.

Look for both mistakes. Only very rarely are golfers too upright or too flat all the way through their swings. Most of the time they are a little bit of both at various points. You will likely be the same.

Ask yourself: Am I under the plane? Am I over the plane? Am I on the plane?

Stand in front of a mirror. Analyze your swing plane based on

FIG. 23 Too flat a backswing (a) forces you to steepen your downswing (b).

a

what I just said. If you hit into the ground too deep, slice to the right, pop up your drives, or tend to hit off the toe, it's a sure bet that you are swinging a steep plane. If you hit off the heel, if you hit shots thin, if you hook the ball, it's equally certain that your downswing plane is flat.

If you are too steep, look first at your backswing. Are you too steep right away? Then steep again on the downswing? Or are you flat going back, then steep coming down? Or are you on plane going back, then steepening your swing coming down? Those are the only options. It is simply a case of locating the introduction of your steepness. Where did it first occur?

More often than not you will find that steepness occurs early in the downswing. Most people take the club back too flat, forcing them to steepen the club on the downswing (see figs. 23a and 23b). In other words, they move the club in, up, then over. "Over the top" is one of

b

the most common mistakes people make. I'm sure you've heard that phrase before!

So start at the beginning. Fix the initial flatness first. Then go on to fix the middle of the swing, the downswing, and the impact. Do it all without a ball. At first, work only on making a better practice swing.

In effect, you are analyzing your error, then trying to do the opposite. That's the way all great teachers teach and the way all great students learn. They analyze what they are doing, then where and how they make their mistake, then try to do the opposite.

If you are taking the club inside, lifting it up, then coming down steep, try to feel like the club is swinging up in the takeaway, flattening a little at the top, then flattening a little more coming down. Reverse your loop.

If you tend to take the club away to the outside and steep, then loop the club to the inside in the downswing so that the club ends up on too flat a plane and approaches the ball on too shallow an arc, try to feel like the club is swinging around you on the takeaway, then up to the top of the backswing and then down in front of you on a steeper plane in the downswing. Again, reverse your loop.

At least at first, exaggerate every move you make. It should all feel very strange. If it doesn't you won't see any difference in your swing. You may think you are doing what you're trying to do, but you probably aren't. So do it more—a lot more—than you first think. Exaggerate. Exaggerate. Exaggerate. You can always back off if you overcook your correction.

USE MIRROR/VIDEO

At this point I usually guide a student through an on-plane swing. I put my hands on him and his club and lead the way through the whole swing. You don't have that luxury. But you do know what above and below the plane looks like. Check yourself in a mirror. Or use a video camera if you have one.

Here's a quick "don't." Don't do what I see so many people doing. They know that their downswings are too steep because they keep sticking the club in the ground. And they know that they have to flatten their downswings. So what do they do?

They take the club away on an even flatter plane on the backswing in an effort to create a flatter downswing. Which, of course, is exactly the opposite of what they should be doing. Do the opposite, not more of the same.

Part Two

Fixing Your Swing

4

The Setup
Preparing to Make Your Move

If you are a regular reader of golf instruction manuals you will probably be surprised to find this area of the game covered this far into the book. Most instruction manuals start with a chapter on "the basics." Or "the fundamentals." Or "the pre-swing." Or "getting into position." Or whatever you want to call the way in which you set your body so that you can hit the ball most effectively. You know the sort of thing I mean. "Good golf starts with a good grip." And so on. Yawn. . . .

This book is different. And for good reason. As I said in the introduction, this is not simply a "how-to" book. This is a fault-fixing book. So far, all of the information on these pages should hopefully have given you a complete understanding of why your golf swing produces the shots that it does. But that is only step one on the way to fixing your faults. The following three chapters represent step two: fixing your swing.

To me, that order of things makes perfect sense. You have to understand what it is you are trying to fix before you can change any aspect of your swing. And the only reason for changing anything in your swing is if you think it will help you hit better shots. I don't change something in a pupil's method just because I don't like the way it looks. I change a setup because it will change a swing for the better, which will then change the flight of the ball. Everything always relates back to the ball-flight and the swing plane.

So never make a change for purely cosmetic reasons. While you may feel that it looks good if, say, your left heel doesn't rise off the ground on your backswing, there is no point in trying to achieve that if it has no beneficial effect on your shots.

FIRST THINGS FIRST

Having said all that, only very rarely do I give a lesson which doesn't involve some type of setup change. The address position has that much influence. Even the slightest shift in your setup will impact your swing.

So the setup is vital. The golf swing is all about action and reaction. Everything you do at address influences the takeaway, which influences the backswing, and so on. It is very much a chain reaction.

Because of this you can work backwards. Make changes to your setup based on what your golf swing is doing. And the great thing is you don't have to be particularly exact in your positioning. Like the swing plane, there is no one setup for everyone. You have some leeway.

For example, the amount you bend forward from the waist at address is not an exact science. If it was, we would all be bent forward, say, twenty-two degrees. But it isn't like that. For some of us maybe twenty degrees is perfect. For others, twenty-one. There's a small range there and as long as you stay within that range you'll be fine. The same is true of knee flex, the angle of your feet, the height of your hands and whether they are a little back or forward. In every area of your setup you have a little room to maneuver, some variance.

Why is posture not exact? The posture you create at address isn't often the one you have at impact. Much of it is feel. You want a consistent starting point, but do you arrive at that same place? Hardly ever. And do you want to? Only if you have a correct swing plane. If you have to, your posture is one place that can adjust the plane for you. That's why it isn't an exact science. Most people don't swing the club on a perfect plane. And if you don't do that, you don't need or want perfect posture.

The best way to check is just to look in a mirror. Get some sequence pictures of a top player from *Golf Digest* and try to set up like Mark O'Meara or Nick Faldo. The worst you'll be is very close to your perfect posture. It doesn't have to be exact. So don't get too wrapped up in it.

There isn't just one way to do things. Let's say you come to me hooking the ball. I might have you stand with your right foot pointed straight ahead and your left foot pointed out more so that you can get your body turning through more (see fig. 24).

Then again, you might be slicing. Let's say your upper body is getting too far ahead of your lower body, leaving the club behind and the face open. Given those factors, I might toe your right foot out a little bit and toe your left foot in compared with the person who hooked the ball (see fig. 25). Still toed-out a little, just not as much. That will get you turning more on the backswing, and encourage more hand and arm action through impact.

There are also little adjustments you can make. If you take the club too much to the inside on the backswing I might move your hands back a little at address. That will encourage the club to move more outside away from the ball. If you tend to take the club back outside the plane I might shift your hands forward at address. All to get the early part of your swing moving more around your body.

FIG. 24 Pointing your left foot out more than your right foot helps you turn through the shot.

FIG. 25 Pointing your right foot out more than your left foot gets you turning more on the backswing.

But, again, nothing is set in stone. Let's say you take the club away to the outside, above the plane. And your hands are ahead of the ball at address. It would be easy to say, "Move your hands back a little." Because it looks better. But doing that will have you taking the club away even more on the outside. So, let me repeat, you don't want to be changing something just for the sake of doing it. Any changes must have some influence on the golf club.

Okay, you've got the message. Not everybody sets up in exactly the same position. There is some leeway at address. Not much, obviously; most great players look pretty similar. But you need to know what it is you're trying to fix before you go messing with your address position.

WHY YOU GET OUT OF POSITION

Most people start off with a pretty good setup, at least in terms of their aim and body positions. But your setup evolves as you hit different shots. If you hit behind the ball a lot, it won't be long before you push your hands forward at address and put the ball further back in your stance. If you slice the ball to the right, you'll close the clubface at address. Same with a hook; the clubface will be set down open at address (see figs. 26a and 26b).

The ball-flight and the impact you create tends to make you change your setup. It changes your aim. It changes the way you stand to the ball. So it isn't enough to say that because you have a good setup you will hit a good shot, or that a bad setup means you will hit a bad shot. But what a bad setup does do is make it harder for you to hit a good shot. You can still do it, but probably not consistently.

It's like when I hear someone say you can't hit a good shot if you can't aim properly. That's nonsense. If you can't hit a straight shot why would you want to aim straight?

Then there is our old friend the grip. Some teachers say you'll never have a good swing without a good grip. But if you don't have a good swing you don't want a good grip. A picture perfect grip is one that matches your swing. When you change anything in your game you need to try to keep that perfect blend if you were already hitting some good shots, or create a perfect blend if you weren't. Any changes should have some influence on the flight of the ball. Sadly, however, that's not how most teaching is done. People change just to be changing.

Don't misunderstand me. There is nothing wrong with building

FIG. 26 Slicers like to close the clubface at address (a); hookers like to open the clubface (b).

good, strong fundamentals. A good setup and a good grip, good alignment, good posture—those are all things which are important. But they don't guarantee good shots. They are just building blocks.

Most of golf instruction is error correction. What are your mistakes? Then correct them. It isn't, put this piece on top of this piece on top of this piece. Yet that is traditionally how golf books have been structured. It's do this, this, this, and this and automatically you'll have a good game at the end of it all.

Not necessarily. For one thing, most students don't want to learn that way. They make, say, four changes, and see no results. So they don't make the fifth change. Every time you make a change you want to see some results. Otherwise, why bother?

If you understand what causes the golf ball to fly in certain directions, you should be able to figure out what you need to change at address to encourage the swing changes that will in turn produce the ball-flight changes you want to effect.

Don't worry so much about making anything perfect. A perfect grip is one that matches your swing. A perfect setup is one that matches your swing. As for the perfect swing, I have yet to see one. No one has ever had a perfect swing and you probably won't be the first. However, you can and will improve. All you have to do is think and practice.

TO BUSINESS

There are only four important aspects in your setup: posture, alignment, stance, and ball position.

Posture is first because the club hits the ball, your hands hold the club, which is attached to your arms, which are attached to your shoulders. So your posture has direct influence on the plane of your swing. Your stance does not. It may have indirect influence—you may stand closed and take the club inside, or stand open and take the club outside—but your shoulders are attached to your arms, so they have direct influence. And that's why posture is the most important.

POSTURE

Okay, let's get specific, or as specific as we can given that none of the following is set in stone. When you stand to the ball you need to bend forward from your hips so that your arms hang down from your shoulders (see fig. 27). You should be in a comfortable position, but one which allows your arms the freedom to swing the club and allows your body to turn easily.

As I said earlier, the bend forward from your hips should be approximately twenty degrees. Your rear end should be stuck out and up a little bit but not too much. It should feel like a ready athletic position, as if you were standing to field a ground ball or shoot a free throw. Your weight should be toward the balls of your feet and evenly distributed between right and left. Your arms hang softly from

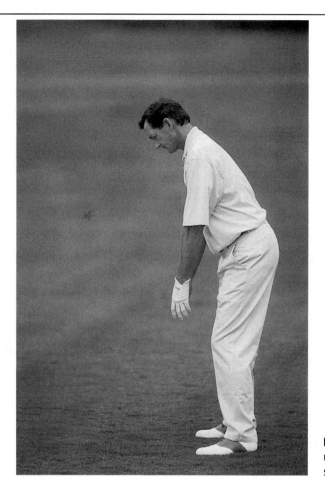

FIG. 27 Bend forward until your arms hang straight down.

your shoulders. There should be no slouching forward from your shoulders. Your upper body should be free of tension, your back fairly straight.

Your lower body, in contrast, is the foundation of your swing. You need some tension there. The lower body should resist as your upper body turns in the backswing, hence the tension. You want to feel a slight tightness on the inside of your legs all the way down to your ankles. Your lower body shouldn't move much on the backswing. Any and all movement should stem from the turning of your upper body pulling your lower body along. Your lower body does not initiate anything in the backswing. That's why you need a solid base, one where your feet are almost fastened to the ground. Imagine if someone were to push you from any direction. If you wouldn't fall over you know you are well balanced (see fig. 28).

FIG. 28 At the top you should be balanced enough to withstand a push from behind.

FIG. 29 A line up the middle of your body should pass through your left eye.

Everything is stacked on top of one another. Your head is on top of your shoulders. Your shoulders are on top of your hips. Your hips are on top of your feet. A line drawn up your back will be angled at about twenty degrees. A line drawn up the center of your body should run right through your left eye (see fig. 29).

That's as good as your posture needs to be to give you a chance to make a good swing. Good posture has a positive influence on your swing, just as bad posture has a negative effect. There are any number of possibilities, but here are a few to ponder.

If you bend forward too much from the hips, your shoulders will

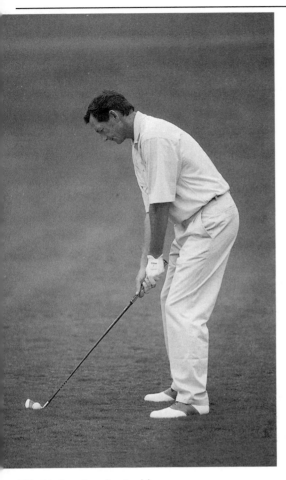 

FIG. 30 Low hands at address . . .   **FIG. 31** sends the club away outside the line.

tilt more than they should as you swing and the club will tend to swing too upright. If you stand up too straight, your shoulders will turn too flat and the club will tend to swing flatter than it should. The more you bend over, the lower your hands will be (see fig. 30). Low hands will send the club away to the outside (see fig. 31). The more you stand up, the higher your hands will be. High hands will tend to make the club move too much to the inside.

See how much even a little postural problem affects the plane of your swing?

ALIGNMENT

Let's start by clearing up a common misconception. Aim and alignment are not the same, they are two different issues. Having good alignment is not the same as having everything—your feet, knees, hips, shoulders, arms, and eyes—aimed at a target.

Aim is taking every aspect of your alignment and aiming it at a specific target. Alignment simply means having everything coordinated and pointing in the same direction. If anything is misaligned, you will have a much greater chance of making a mistake in your takeaway.

With good alignment, aiming is easy. Especially if you hit straight shots. You have to have good alignment to hit good shots. But you don't need good aim. Proper aim is what gets your straight shots to go to a specific target.

Aiming, in fact, is easy. If you don't believe me ask a friend who has never played golf before to hold a club and aim at a target in the distance. I bet he does it perfectly. Beginners always do. They all aim at the target until they have hit a couple of shots. Only then do they start to adjust. Let's say they slice the first three balls. Guess where they will aim for the fourth one? That's correct; to the left. All to compensate for the left-to-right curve on the ball.

In contrast, with good alignment you have a great opportunity to make a good swing and hit a good shot. Maybe it won't be to the target you thought you were aiming at, but it will still be a good, solidly struck shot. If you can do that on a consistent basis, you will soon find your aim.

Why all the confusion? Because there are too many teaching philosophies. Some teachers say you can't hit straight if you can't aim straight. My idea is that if you can't hit straight, why would you ever want to aim straight? Plus, if you curve your shots, the amount of curve is going to be different for every club in the bag. They all have different lofts, so they all impart differing amounts of sidespin on the ball. So if you have a curvature problem, aiming is next to impossible.

During a lesson I never ask a pupil to pick out a target. Only after he has hit a few shots will I ask him where he thinks he is aiming. I just watch him hit and look at his alignment. At least initially, aim isn't a big concern.

All I want to see are good shots, so the first priority is always to get you hitting good shots straight to where you are aimed, wherever that may be. Remember, ball-flight is everything, so any mistake with ball-flight is where you start correcting. If you hook or slice, you are going to have aiming problems. But get your alignment right and you have a better chance to make a good takeaway and a good swing and hit a good shot. And aim better.

Ideally, you want to take the club back right along the angle of the clubshaft as it was at address. That is the start of a neutral, on-plane swing, something which is easier to achieve if you have good posture and good alignment.

Lining Up

Proper alignment is easy to describe. You want to have your feet, knees, thighs, hips, arms, shoulders, and eyes all lined up parallel left of your target. That would be proper alignment. The bend in your right elbow makes up for the fact that your right hand is lower on the club than your left and closer to the ball, which keeps your shoulders and arms parallel with everything else.

Most important is the fact that they are coordinated correctly. Whenever students ask me where they are aiming I invariably have to wonder which part of the body they are referring to. Their feet might be closed. Their shoulders might be open. Their eyes might be angled left or right. They are pointed in so many different directions that it's difficult for me to know where they are aiming.

The most important aspects of alignment are the shoulders, arms, and eyes. Your feet are important, but nowhere near as important as the other parts of your body. They receive more attention than they warrant considering their relation to the golf club.

What you may not know is that your eyes have a big influence on your swing. If you set up with them aligned to the right, you will probably swing that way. If you tilt your head more one way or the other, you'll probably swing too steeply or too flat. You want to keep your eyes level to the ground and parallel to the target line (see fig. 32). That's important for your balance and for the direction and angle of your golf swing. All because that is the way we function. Our whole world is based on being level to the horizon. When you start tilting your eyes you run into equilibrium problems, which makes it hard for you even to put the club correctly on the ground behind the ball, never mind hit it squarely.

Almost everyone who reverse pivots swings the club back so that their eyes are at an angle looking down at the ground. If they kept their eyes level, they wouldn't reverse pivot. That's how I fix that

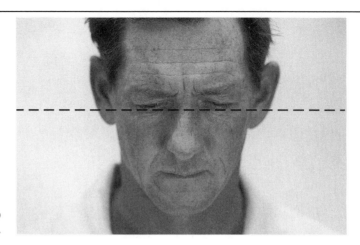

FIG. 32 At address, keep your eyes level.

problem. Use the brim of your hat or the top of your sunglasses to check how level your eyes are throughout the swing.

One last thought. If you have watched Jack Nicklaus play golf over the years you have probably noticed how he always lines up on an intermediate target about a yard in front of his ball. The theory is that it is easier to align the clubface with something that close as opposed to a flag 200 yards away (see fig. 33). I like that method. Try it.

FIG. 33 Lining up a spot a yard in front of the ball can help your alignment.

Create Good Alignment

Put a club down on the ground so that you can line up your feet (fig. 34). Then hold another club across your legs, just above your knees (fig. 35). Use the club on the ground as a reference. When the two are parallel, your legs are aligned. Moving up, lay the club across your hips, aligning them (fig. 36). Then your shoulders (fig. 37) and eyes (fig. 38). If you have been aligned badly, you'll be amazed at the different feel you have.

Now, set up to the ball. Your right hand is closer to the ball than your left. Your right elbow is bent. Don't overdo it, though. I see many people tucking their right elbows in more than they need to. That only aligns your arms to the right, which will encourage you to take the club away too much on the inside, then loop it over on the

FIG. 34 Line up your feet with a club along your toes.

FIG. 35 Then check your knees . . .

FIG. 36 your hips . . .

FIG. 37 your shoulders . . .

FIG. 38 and your eyes.

FIG. 39 At address, the toe of your club should be slightly off the ground.

downswing. Your arms should be parallel to the target line. If your right arm was perfectly straight, your arms would be lined up to the left. Try it and you'll see what I mean.

So you're set up. Your right shoulder should be just a little lower than your left shoulder—again because your right hand is lower on the club. But no more or less than the amount your right hand is lower than your left hand on the club.

You must align your body and the clubface together. The face must sit at right angles to your body lines. That is perfect alignment. Now you have given yourself a chance.

A point in passing. At address the toe of the club should be up just off the ground. When you swing, the shaft bends two ways; it arches down and back. When the shaft bows down during the downswing the lie angle flattens slightly. So a properly fitted club will have the toe up a little bit at address (see fig. 39).

THE STANCE

Let's say you are hitting a 5-iron. At address your feet should be shoulder width apart (see fig. 40). By your feet I mean that a line drawn down from the outside of your shoulders would pass through the middle of your heels.

In general, because you eventually want to turn through and face the target, your left foot should be toed out a little more than your

FIG. 40 A shoulder-width stance is best for a 5-iron.

right foot. The right foot is square to just slightly toed out; the left foot just a little more. Those foot positions help your lower body resist on the backswing and help you turn through into the follow-through.

But there are variations depending on your ball-flight. In general, people who hook the golf ball may want to toe out a little more with the left foot and keep the right foot perfectly square. They need to get the lower body moving in the forward swing and this helps.

People who slice might benefit from toeing the left foot in a bit and the right foot out a little more. If you are trying to shape shots, that will help make it easier also. An adjustment in your stance has the possibility to influence what your body does and so affect the hands and arms and, in turn, the club. Okay, so it's indirect, and a certain stance position certainly doesn't guarantee a certain shape of shot. But it can help. And it is an easy adjustment to make.

Wider/Narrower

As the clubs get longer, your stance widens. As to what is the width of your widest and narrowest stances, I wouldn't claim to know exactly. But it is no more than a couple of inches either way. It's a feel thing.

If you stand too wide you are going to have too much body movement. If your stance is on the narrow side you will promote more of a hands and arms swing. But if you do move your body at all, you will lose your balance.

When you widen your stance you lower your center of gravity and move your center back behind the ball more. This will help you make more of a sweeping motion. The driver is the club for which you need the most help with that, because the ball is teed up off the ground.

The closer you stand, the narrower your stance will be, the more your center line will be forward, and the more your center of gravity will rise. All of which helps you create more of a downward motion. Perfect for short irons.

A chip shot would be your narrowest stance, because you want to hit down on the ball.

BALL POSITION

Let the design of the club in your hands dictate where you position the ball within your stance.

On a driver the shaft goes straight into the head and the face progresses in front of the shaft. So your hands are going to be even or a little behind the ball (see fig. 41).

With a 5-iron the shaft is now slightly in front of the clubface. That's how it was made. So even though your arms are the same in terms of being in front of your body, you have a narrower stance. You are not trying to make a straight line with your left arm and the club. This is another misconception. That straight line should be there at impact, but not at address. You're not getting ready to make impact; you're getting ready to make a backswing. (The backswing is

FIG. 41 For a driver, your hands should be slightly behind the ball.

going to set you up for the downswing, which will set you up for impact. At address your weight is 50–50 between your left and right foot, with a driver maybe 45–55. But when you get to impact most of your weight will be on your left side. This business of trying to create impact at address is just not right.)

So the ball position has, in effect, moved back for the 5-iron. If you put the clubhead on the ground behind a ball and let the club sit just the way it was made to, then make your triangle with your hands and arms in front of your body, the ball will find its correct position.

When you get to the sand wedge, the shortest club and the one whose shaft is the most in front of its head, the ball will be as far back as it is going to get. But it will still be ahead of center (see fig. 42). The ball doesn't move more than about two or three inches over the whole set from driver to sand wedge. But it does change (see fig. 43).

FIG. 42 Even for a sand wedge, the ball is still ahead of center within your stance.

FIG. 43 The change in ball position from sand wedge to driver is no more than a couple of inches.

FIG. 44 Pushers and hookers of the ball are generally more comfortable hitting Ball A. Pullers and slicers invariably prefer Ball C. Both, of course, should be trying to hit Ball B.

The constant in the setup is the triangle formed by your arms, hands, and shoulders. That is constant. It doesn't change. The ball position changes because your clubs are made differently (see fig. 44).

THE WAGGLE

I always include the waggle when I talk about the setup. A good waggle sets you up to make a good swing. It's a mini practice swing. So it's one of the more important parts of the swing. You are practicing your takeaway (see fig. 45).

FIG. 45 Think of the waggle as practicing your takeaway.

A waggle is also good because it can relax you. It can "pace" your swing and help with your rhythm and tempo. When you waggle the club be specific. Waggle it on plane. Waggle it right along the angle of the shaft, the clubface just opening slightly.

Waggle with your hands. Not with your arms or your shoulders. Soften your hands. Feel a slight upward cocking motion of your wrists along with just a little rotation of the left forearm and hand. Feel a looseness to encourage smoothness in your swing. And practice taking the club back on plane. It's really important.

PRE-SHOT ROUTINE

For a long time this was one of the most neglected parts of the game. Not anymore. Nowadays I hear many players and teachers talking about the importance of a consistent pre-shot routine. And that's good. What I don't hear, however, are some specifics. What exactly should you be doing in the last seconds before adopting your address position? And how long should it take?

FIG. 46 Standing behind the ball, look at your target and visualize your ball-flight.

FIG. 47 Walk forward to the ball still thinking of the ball flying to the hole.

The best way to answer both those questions is to describe my own pre-shot routine. It isn't definitive because we are all different. The key is to build yourself a routine that works for you. Then stick with it. Do it every time you hit a shot on the course.

Here's how mine works. It takes fifteen seconds from start to finish.

FIG. 48 Align the clubface with the hole . . .   **FIG. 49** then take your stance.

The Setup

FIG. 50 Glance up at the target . . .

FIG. 51 then look at the ball . . .

FIG. 52 then waggle with your hands.

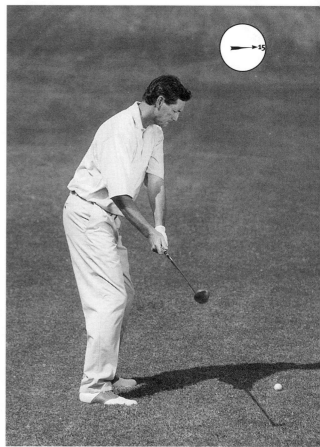

FIG. 53 Start your swing.

5

Body, Hands and Arms, or Both?

Ever since man started taking an interest in finding the most efficient way to strike a little white ball around a big field with a stick, there have been disagreements about how to best achieve that end. Within those squabbles, two camps have evolved, at least when it comes to the full swing. There are those who feel that if you turn your body correctly the hands and arms will swing correctly. Others take the opposite view; the hands and arms swinging correctly will lead to a correct turning of the body.

In fact, when you talk about teaching these days all you hear is body versus hands and arms. To me, this is just fixing a hook versus fixing a slice (see chapter 6). For example, Ben Hogan's book, *The Modern Fundamentals of Golf,* is one of the greatest ever written. But I've always thought it was mistitled. It should be called, *How Not to Hook* by Ben Hogan.

Early in his career Hogan was a terrible hooker. He says stuff like "from the top of your swing your hands actively do nothing." Or "turn your left hip out of the way and that leads your downswing." Well, give that information to a slicer and he'll slice even more.

Still, nothing in golf stays the same for long. "Body" teachers and those who emphasize the hands and arms have each held sway at various times over the last five decades. As the game evolves, so does teaching and the way students learn.

For example, twenty-five years ago most teachers, led by the likes of Bob Toski, John Jacobs, and Jim Flick, placed heavy emphasis on the hands and arms. The teaching philosophies of those men, all great instructors, evolved from golf schools where they taught the game to the masses of golfers, most of whom slice.

Then things changed. Largely due to the influence of David Leadbetter and his work with Nick Faldo and other tour pros, "body teaching" became fashionable in the mid–1980s. And that was how things stayed for a few years.

Today's teaching isn't dominated by the instructors who work with average players. The most influential teachers don't work in golf schools anymore. The highest profile instructors are those working with tour pros. And this influences the way the swing is taught.

Typically, tour pros have great hands. They use their hands in the swing much better than the average player. Which is why nearly every great player has fought a hook at some time or another in his career. Poor players have never done that. They rarely hook. They hit pulls and call them hooks but they don't start shots off to the right and hook the ball too much to the left. They just don't hit true hooks.

Great players fight a hook because they have fast hands. Some may not think so, but all of them still have a lot of hand action in the hit at the bottom of their swings. So in their thinking they place more emphasis on the motion of the body. Why? Because hand action isn't something they have to think about. They already have great hands. So they focus on the body. They feel like they need to get the body to go along with the hands and arms to (a) get their timing right and (b) get the feeling of taking their hands "out" of the swing.

Even when they have achieved the feeling of taking the hands "out" of the swing, tour pros still have much more hand action than the average player. They like to feel that they are hitting more with the body than the hands and arms. The idea that the big muscles will be more productive under pressure than the smaller muscles has come about because it corresponds with the feeling the tour pros are looking for.

Which is fine. Emphasizing the big muscles could very well be the way to teach the typical touring pro, but it isn't necessarily the way to work with a 15-handicapper who slices. Extra emphasis on his body will only make him slice more. He needs more of a hands and arms swing.

FIND YOUR STYLE

Hands and arms teachers have always been "king of the hill" longer than their body counterparts. There's a simple reason for this: Hands and arms teachers are typically dedicated to teaching the masses. And the masses slice. In fact, over 90 percent of golfers slice. And they slice because they don't have great hand and arm action. They tend to hit too much with their big muscles and not enough with their small muscles. They hit with their shoulders; they hit with their bodies. In fact, they often use everything but the golf club to hit the ball. And unfortunately, the greater effort they put into their swings doesn't translate to greater power.

When you hit with your hands and arms, your hands are the primary power sources in your golf swing. They are the fastest parts of your body involved in the swing. So your hands can produce a lot of speed. Great athletes have great hands.

In golf, that's one way to create clubhead speed. There are others. I've heard people say that Tiger Woods hits the ball so far because of the speed of his hips. His hips are fast because he's fast. His shoulders are fast. His hands are fast. Everything is fast. He has fast muscles and great strength to support those muscles, not to mention a great swing. That's why he hits it a long way.

But great hands produce more speed. Most people don't have either. They don't even use their hands to produce the speed they are capable of producing. The clubface doesn't square up quick enough, so the ball slices to the right.

That simple fact did much to popularize the theory that the hands and arms led the body. Teachers still taught people to turn their bodies, of course. But that wasn't what the vast majority of their pupils needed. So the focus inevitably shifted to the hands and arms.

BLEND THE TWO

Let's break this all down. Do you need a better body rotation or a better hands and arms motion in your swing? As we've seen, this argument goes on and on and on. But there are great teachers on both sides. That makes me think that each has merit.

Both are correct. Both are important. Both are influential. In fact, even the teachers who talk more about the body still teach a lot of hands and arms. A body teacher fixes a slice by getting the student to swing his hands and arms. And the hands and arms guy fixes a hook by getting the pupil to move his body a little better.

It's safe to say you have to move your body relatively well, or you won't be able to swing your hands and arms. And if you swing your hands and arms well, but don't move your body, you won't be great either. You have to have a good blend of the two.

When I look at a swing, I always look at the club. What is the club doing wrong in the swing? How do I get it to do something better? What is making this club swing in an improper direction or angle? What is making it do something wrong? Is it the body? Or is it the hands and arms?

In fact, it is usually a bit of both. For example, it's absurd to think that if you turn your body correctly then the hands and arms will automatically swing the club on the proper plane. You could turn your body at a good angle. You could turn on the proper plane. You could keep your posture. You could do everything right. Yet you could still swing your hands and arms any way you wanted to. Sure, they might have more of a tendency to swing in the right place, but there is no guarantee.

Equally, swinging your hands and arms on the proper plane does not guarantee a proper body motion. You can't make those statements. Both work together. But both work independently, too. So you have to deal with each depending on what your tendencies are.

BODY FIRST

You do need a certain amount of correctness in the way your body sets up to the golf ball and in the way your body pivots. If you don't you won't be able to swing your hands and arms on the correct plane. In fact, the body motion is often the first thing I fix in any swing. If the body motion is very far off, improving the swing of the hands and arms won't fix it. For example, no hands and arms swing thought is going to totally fix a reverse pivot—your upper body turning in front of the golf ball, rather than behind it (see fig. 54). But if the body motion is only a little bit off, a better hands and arms action might help.

Not turning your shoulders or hips enough isn't that big an issue compared with the plane of the swing. As we've seen, the plane of your swing determines how you hit the ball—or a combination of posture and plane. They feed off one another. If you don't have one correct, you can't have the other. If you swing on too steep a plane you have to come out of your posture. If you don't you'll stick the club in the ground. And that's where the stalemate arises. Some say that the loss of posture results from the upright swing; others contend that the upright swing results from the loss of posture. Deadlock.

That's why I fix the body motion mistakes that have a more direct influence on the hands and arms swing. Then I go after the hands and arms.

FIG. 54 Turning in front of the ball is a reverse pivot.

Your ball-flight mistake dictates what school of thought you need. If you slice you need a decent body motion on the backswing, but your hit needs to be applied more by your hands and arms. A hooker needs a good body motion, but if you don't swing the club on the correct plane you will tend to overuse your hands coming through. So it works both ways.

Everything is geared toward getting the golf club to swing on the correct plane.

When you set up, you need to get yourself centered over the ball. Given that, as you turn back your upper body turns as your lower body resists (see fig. 55). You have tension on the inside of your legs. You turn your upper body back and try to turn your shoulders about twice as much as your hips. That's not written in stone—some people aren't that flexible so they need to turn their hips more—and that's okay, but if you are capable of making that full shoulder turn with half as much hip turn, that's ideal.

A good turn creates tension, a kind of wind-up effect. When you turn back you'll find your weight shift to the inside of your right heel. Your shoulders are turning and you feel resistance all the way up the inside of your right leg. You'll feel a pulling or stretching on the left side of your back. At the top it should feel as if you can't maintain your position for more than a couple of seconds.

If you get to the top and can stay there for twenty seconds, you surely don't have maximum coil in your golf swing. There is a difference between making a lot of turn and making a turn that is coiled. If you coil you create more power because you can unwind faster. And you'll unwind more automatically.

So it isn't just how much turn you make. There is nothing that says you have to turn your shoulders ninety degrees. Equally, there is nothing saying that more than ninety degrees is wrong. What really counts is how correct your turn is.

As for your left heel, in an ideal world it should stay flat on the ground. But if that is the only way you can make a proper turn, let it come up off the ground. Take care though. Lifting the left heel tends

FIG. 55 Your lower body resists in the backswing.

to make everything lift up. If you do that you will have a change in your posture. Keep the bend from your hips. If your back is angled twenty degrees at address, at the top of your swing the angle of your shoulders will be twenty degrees to the ground. Stay centered and keep your posture the same. Those are the things you are looking for from your body.

Your right knee should stay kicked in a little bit. You don't want to slide to the outside of your right foot. You are, in effect, turning around your right leg while staying fairly centered. If you are going to move, you want to move your right, not your left. I like to see players moving right or staying centered. There is nothing wrong with moving your head laterally a little. You can always move forward on the downswing. But you don't want to turn and lean toward the target in the backswing.

Roll in with your left foot so that the weight moves to the inside. But don't let your knee move much. When your left knee kicks in a lot, you're asking for a reverse pivot. Your knee only moves in at all because your shoulders pull it. Your lower body needs to feel as if it is moving only because your upper body is pulling it along. Your lower body does nothing by itself on the backswing. Build coil. Then, everything happens in reverse on the downswing. Your lower body pulls your upper body along with it.

If you happen not to be too flexible, don't worry so much about coil on your backswing. With lack of flexibility comes coil. If you're very flexible, you have to achieve this coiling motion. If you're already tight, you're already coiled up, albeit restricted.

If that is the case, and you could use a little more turn, give your body some help. Toe your right foot out a little. Let your left foot come up a little. Let your hips turn a little more. Those things will all give you more turn and more arc. Once again, there is no rule saying you have to turn ninety degrees. It is the quality of the turn that counts. You can swing the club on the correct plane with half a turn or a full turn. Besides, how much turn you make is more a factor in power than in accuracy.

If you are used to making a ninety degree turn, then all of a sudden you only make a seventy-five degree turn, your timing and rhythm will be thrown off. This tends to happen under pressure. Tension can shorten your turn and throw your timing off. The result is a bad shot.

If you always turn seventy-five degrees and always swing on plane, you're going to hit many great shots. They won't be as powerful as they would be if you could turn ninety degrees, but that sort of accuracy is still pretty good.

HOLDING THE CLUB

Uh-oh, here comes the grip part. The grip is boring and the last thing anyone wants to change. But, as every golf book ever written will tell you, it is important. For the record, here is how to take hold of the club.

I like to see the club running at an angle across the left hand, from just underneath the palm of the hand through the first knuckle of the forefinger (see fig. 56). When you close your hand I want to see the thumb and forefinger pressed together to form a "V." They should be pinched together, not apart (see fig. 57).

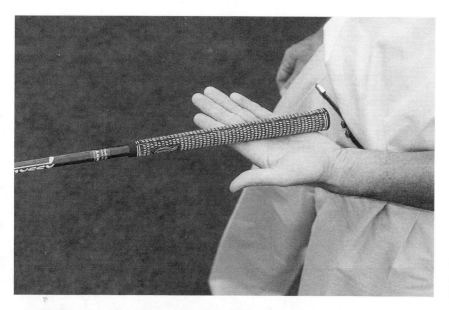

FIG. 56 The club runs diagonally across your left hand.

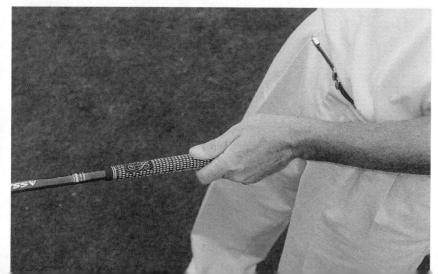

FIG. 57 Your thumb and forefinger form a "V."

When you take your grip, pinch both thumbs into your forefingers. That's a good start to any grip.

The right-hand grip is more in your fingers (see figs. 58a and 58b). The most important part of the grip is that your hands fit together properly and that they work as a unit (see fig. 59). Your grip pressure should be even in both hands. Golf isn't a left- or right-handed game; it's a both-handed game.

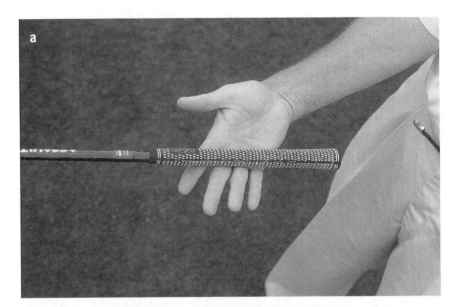

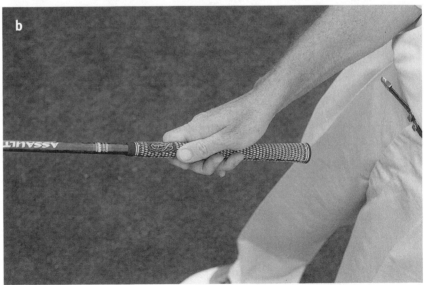

FIG. 58 Hold the club mainly in the fingers of your right hand (a), then again make your "V" (b).

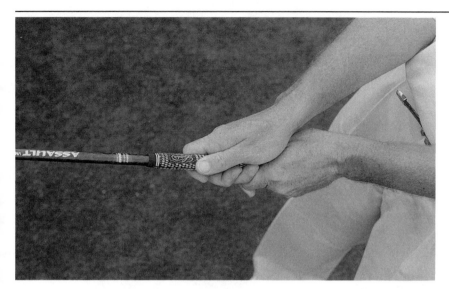

FIG. 59 Maintain an even grip pressure in both hands.

How tightly you hold the club depends on your ball-flight. People who slice tend to hold on too tight; those who hook, too soft. So, to correct a hook, hold on tighter. To correct a slice, hold on softer. What you usually read is that a light hold on the club is best. But that's good advice only if you slice. It's not so good if you hook.

I prefer the overlapping grip. People who interlock tend to put the little finger of the right hand all the way in, which puts the right hand in a really bad position—too far underneath the club in a strong position.

Overlap, Interlock, or Ten-Finger?

To be honest, I don't really care. And neither should you (see figs. 60, 61, and 62). The style of your grip isn't that important. As long as your grip is close to orthodox, it doesn't really matter.

A good grip gives you the flexibility in your wrists to let them hinge and unhinge during the swing. A neutral grip gives you the best chance to keep the club on plane. If you have a good swing, of course. An off-plane swing requires that you have a less than neutral grip. Your grip must match your swing.

So it's important that your hands fit on the club in a way which allows your wrists to hinge easily and freely. And that your grip matches your swing. Think about that. People say you can't have a good swing if you don't have a good grip, but as I've said, if you don't have a good swing you don't want a good grip.

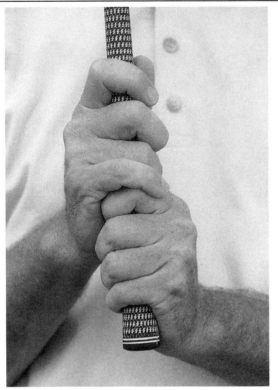

FIG. 60 Overlapping . . .

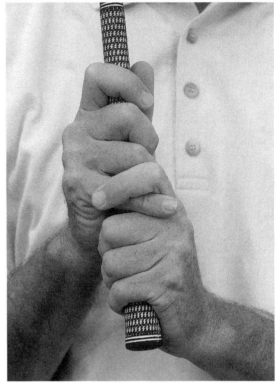

FIG. 61 . . . Interlocking . . .

FIG. 62 . . . Ten-finger . . .

Doesn't matter. Go with
the grip you are most
comfortable with.

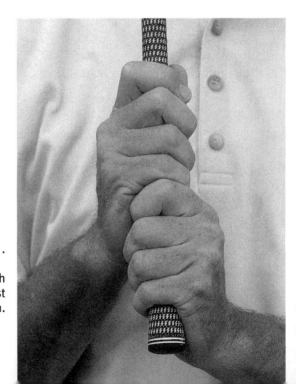

I never change someone's grip unless they can't hold onto the club, or they can't cock their wrists, or if the ball tells me to. In other words, if you are hooking the ball and you have a strong grip, or if you are slicing and have a weak grip, then it is time to change your hold on the club. Other than that, don't mess with it.

Stronger Grips

Grips have generally gotten stronger over the last fifteen years and it's because of the way most teachers have gone about trying to fix the better players' mistakes.

When a good player gets the club stuck behind him on the down-swing, he tends to flip his hands over the ball through impact and hit a hook. There is a difference between the club being stuck behind and coming too much from the inside. You could be coming too much from the inside and yet still have the club in front of you. Or you could have the club coming too much from behind you and also too much inside. These are two different mistakes with totally different corrections.

As soon as teachers saw the club getting stuck behind a good player, they said he had to swing the club more left. I guess they were hoping that the club would come down in front of the player and swing to the left. If it had, everything might have been fine. But to get the club going left, most players rotated their bodies more through the ball and now everything was going left. Unfortunately, the club was still stuck behind him, the clubface open because his upper body was out in front of the ball. Suddenly good players were hitting the ball straight right and high.

The root cause was an old videotape of Ben Hogan. His club swung off to the left through impact. Everyone looked and saw the club exiting to the left past the ball. But who cares about that? Not me. First things first. What about the ball? Where is it going?

Anyway, to fix this new high right shot something had to be done, and that's where the stronger grips came from. They are compensations for improper corrections to an earlier mistake. By the way, if you go with a strong grip to fix the "straight-right" shot, you also have to accept a lower ball-flight. When you hit with the shoulders in an effort to swing left, your right shoulder is right on top of the ball, delofting the club. This is why some good players can't get the ball up in the air and are having a hard time hitting a draw that starts to the right.

Neutral

A neutral grip is one where, at the top of the swing, the left wrist and the clubface are parallel (see fig. 63a). That's how you check your grip. Not just by looking in the mirror at address. Check out the top of your swing also. How does the clubface look? If the face is toe down, your grip is probably too weak or your left wrist is cupped

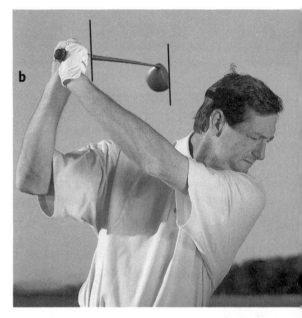

FIG. 63 Your grip is neutral when the back of your left wrist and the clubface are parallel at the top of the swing (a). Too weak a grip or a cupped wrist will have the face "open" at the top (b); too strong a grip or a bowed wrist will put the face in a "closed" position (c).

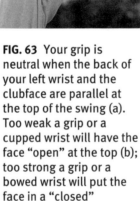

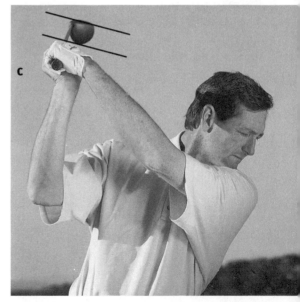

(see fig. 63b). If the face is looking skyward, your grip is probably too strong or your left wrist is bowed (see fig. 63c). If your grip was good when you started and your club is on plane with your left wrist flat to your left forearm, your clubface should be square. If the clubface is open or closed at the top, then you have let go of the grip and it has moved in your hands somewhere on the backswing.

But you only want a neutral grip if you have a good swing. Other than that, you want a slight adjustment one way or the other. Because a majority of people slice and need some extra distance, a slightly stronger grip is what they need.

HANDS AND ARMS

Now that you have a firm hold on the club and understand how your body turns, let's take a look at the hands and arms and how they relate to the plane of the swing. If you take the club back away from the ball a few parts have to work together. Your shoulders turn, as we've already covered. And your wrists hinge as if your hands are going straight up and down.

Cock your wrists up and down as if you are hammering a nail or casting a fishing pole (see fig. 64). The clubshaft should be vertical in

FIG. 64 Cock the club up with your wrists as you start the swing.

FIG. 65 Turn your
shoulders, swing your
arms back and up as you
rotate your left forearm,
and cock your wrists up.

front of your nose—if you don't do anything but cock your wrists up. Now turn your shoulders as you swing your arms back and up, rotating your left forearm as you go (see fig. 65). When you get those four things working together the clubface gradually opens to stay square to the plane and the arc of your swing. If your arm doesn't rotate, the shaft will be too steep. You have to rotate your arm to get the club on the plane.

As for what you should focus on, it depends on your mistake.

If your shaft tends to be too upright away from the ball, ask yourself why. Is it because of your body? Are your shoulders tilting and changing your posture? Are your arms swinging straight up and not around? Or is it a lack of rotation in your left arm?

If the club is too flat, is your body turning too quickly, pulling you to the inside? That could be because your lower body isn't resisting. Or is it because your arms and hands are pulling to the inside? Or is it because your hands and/or arms are rotating too much at some point in your backswing?

QUESTIONS

At this stage I always get a number of questions from students. Here are the more common ones:

What should the backswing feel like?

Keep your upper body pivoting on the posture you set up on and resist with your lower half. Let your left arm gradually rotate as it swings up and back. Let your wrists hinge up at the same time and make sure your arms stay in front of you as you swing the club back to the top of the swing.

When should my wrists cock?

Immediately. But gradually. Nothing says you can't cock them fully right away, but the danger is getting too narrow a backswing. If I see someone who cocks their wrists right away, I don't necessarily change that. Seve Ballesteros does it really quickly. John Cook does it late. Neither is right; neither is wrong. If I changed either I'd be teaching personal preference.

As I see it, in a perfect takeaway the wrist cock should be gradual. Your wrists hinge as your shoulders turn. A quarter of the way into your backswing you should have a quarter of your wrist cock, a quarter of your shoulder turn, a quarter of your arm swing, and a quarter of your forearm rotation. But as long as you are swinging on your plane and your body is pivoting correctly, you can do all four whenever you want during the backswing. Late or early. There are plusses and minuses to both. Early may get a little narrow. Late may make you "flippy" from the top.

When does the club come up?

The club comes up immediately. The arc of the swing is such that the club is on the ground only at address and impact. Everywhere else the club is either coming up or going down. You bend over from your hips, so now your left shoulder turns under slightly and your right shoulder moves up. That happens immediately, so the club has to come off the ground. For it to stay on the ground you either have to turn too level, overextend your arms, or drag the club too much to the inside.

Should I take the club back inside or straight back?

Low and straight back doesn't work because you are standing to the side of the ball. You don't have to worry about the fact that the club moves to the inside. As long as your arms stay "connected" to your body, and you turn, your club will move to the inside. The challenge is in getting the club to come up the correct amount as it moves inside. Straight back is off the plane.

Should I take the club back slow?

Not necessarily. You should take the club back at the speed that is natural for you as an individual. Concentrate on the correctness rather than the speed of your takeaway. The only time I tell a student to slow down is when he isn't giving himself time to think about what he is doing.

TRANSITION FROM BACKSWING TO DOWNSWING

The key here is creating enough separation between your arms and body at the top of your swing. It is crucial that the relationship between your hands, arms, and body stays the same as your upper body turns on the backswing.

Most people are too quick with the right side in transition. Maybe they are quick because they take the club too far inside on the backswing. Or because they turned too quick with the right side going back. Or because they swung back on too flat a plane and are now coming over the top in the downswing. Or because they have a tendency to slice and are trying to stop the ball going to the right.

That's why people tend to have trouble with the transition. The thought and the feel should be that as you get to the top of the swing your upper body is "staying" there as your arms and the golf club start to drop (see fig. 66). As that happens, you make a lateral motion with your hips toward the target. You have to transfer your weight. Most of your weight is on the inside of your right heel at the top. The lateral motion is at the same angle as your hips are at the top of the backswing. At the start of the downswing your weight moves from the inside of your right heel to your left toe.

FIG. 66 From the top, let your arms and the club "drop."

That sounds complicated and, yes, it can be. But it can also be simple. What you need to think and feel depends again on your ball-flight mistake. Which is what our next chapter is all about.

THE DOWNSWING

When you set up, your arms are out in front of you. When you turn, your arms stay in front of you. That is a key to making a correct turn. You turn back and through keeping the relationship between your arms and your body the same.

By staying out in front of you, your hands and arms give your backswing width. Your turn also helps in that regard. When you come back down, you reverse what you did on the backswing. Your arms have rotated, so on the downswing they must lower and rotate back to your side. It is the rotation of your arms down into your body which gets the club out in front of you coming down. Rotate on the way back, then reverse the process.

As you swing the club down, your lower body starts to shift forward and weight transfers from your right heel to your left toe in the downswing. That lateral motion is important in setting your swing to the inside on the downswing. And remember: that move must start from the ground up. As your hips continue to turn, your weight follows and shifts across the outside of your left foot and into your left heel, which is where it is at impact.

As the club contacts the ball the back of your left hand squares up. If you're like most people, this needs to be an active thought. You need to feel the back of the hand squaring up. It is as if you are slapping something with the back of your left hand (see fig. 67). You

FIG. 67 "Slap" impact with the back of your left hand.

want your forearm and the back of your left hand to arrive at the ball at the same time, as if they are hitting into a wall.

Think of the back of your left hand as the clubface. At impact you want it flat and facing the target. If you hit with your knuckles up you are adding loft. If you hit with the side of your hand you are leaving the face open. If you turn your hand over the face will be closed. Turning your knuckles down delofts the club.

In effect, your arm is rotating and your wrists are releasing. The cocking they did on the way back needs to be released as the club swings through the ball. Uncocking your wrists and rotating the arm represents the release of the club through the ball. If you slice this needs to be a conscious thought. Hogan called it supination.

THE FOLLOW-THROUGH

If you swing on the correct plane on the backswing and downswing, it is relatively easy to stay on plane to the end of your follow-through.

But don't neglect your follow-through. Although the ball has already been hit, the follow-through and finish are important parts of your golf swing. You might work from the start of your swing to the finish most of the time, but you can do the opposite and still achieve some great results. A thought, feeling, or image of your finish position can often change your entire swing.

You can change your backswing or your downswing by thinking about the follow-through. There is nothing wrong with focusing first on getting your follow-through on plane. Golf swings can be fixed from either end. The picture of a certain finish can even influence your takeaway. If I tell a pupil to swing more to the right on the through swing, it isn't long before he starts taking the club away to the inside on the backswing—even though I said not one word about the backswing.

Here's where your club and body should move through impact and into your finish. It's simple really. The plane of your swing in the through swing should be a mirror image of the backswing and the downswing. Your club, hands, and arms reach a point of extension past the ball, the club passing through the point where it is simultaneously parallel to the target-line and the ground (see fig. 68). As you reach that point of extension, your left arm begins to bend as your right arm extends in the opposite way it did in the backswing.

As for your body, it continues to rotate through the shot, your hips

FIG. 68 In the follow-
through your left arm
bends as your right arm
extends.

leading your shoulders. Your hands and arms stay in front of your body just as they did in the backswing. The plane of your through swing is a mirror image of your backswing.

At the finish your hips have turned so that they are at least perpendicular to the target-line, with your shoulders perpendicular to the target-line, but never beyond that point. Your elbows should both be bent, your wrists re-cocked and the club across your neck and back.

A "hook-finish" would see your body through less, your hands and arms all the way through and the clubshaft pointing down, closer to perpendicular. A "slice-finish" would see your right side through more, the club pointed more parallel to the ground or even up in the air and less re-cocking of your wrists.

So work on your swing in both directions—from the start to the finish and from the finish back to the start.

6

Straightening Your Slice or Your Hook

As with so many other things in the golf swing, there are only three possibilities when it comes to the shape of a shot: straight, slice, or hook. And not many of us hit perfectly straight shots. Almost everyone tends to hit their shots either from right-to-left or left-to-right—hooks and slices.

When I look at a pupil, I know very quickly whether he has a tendency to hook or slice. In fact, even if you do hit the ball pretty straight you will have a tendency to curve one way more than the other, and when you do have to curve a shot you will find one or the other easier to play. I always ask players who insist that they hit their shots dead straight, "If you were standing on the last hole and had to hit a shot for the Open and couldn't go over or under the tree but around it, which way would you go? Would you hook it or slice it?" The answer tells you which play is your normal shot (see fig. 69).

Mark O'Meara has a great golf swing, but he would elect to draw it around the tree. Nick Faldo also has a great swing, yet he would probably go for the fade. Mark's bad shot comes when his draw turns into a pull-hook; Nick's bad shot comes when his fade turns into a push-slice. So no matter how great the swing, there is always a tendency to fight one shot or the other. Or one shot is at least easier to play (see figs. 70 and 71).

One way to keep yourself "in the middle" is by learning the "other" shot. You should always spend at least some of your practice time working shots in the opposite direction from your natural tendency.

105

FIG. 69 Would you hook
. . . or slice?

For example, Sam Snead was asked once what he did when he was slicing shots on the course. He said he played with the left-to-right ball-flight on the course, then went to the range and tried to hit hooks for an hour. The same was true when Sam was troubled by a hook. He'd play with it on the course, then go hit slices for an hour.

If you can play both shots intentionally, with the same amount of curve and the same trajectory, with equal ease, then you have the most neutral golf swing ever (turn pro immediately). But, in reality, everyone finds one shot easier than the other, if they don't fight one.

FIG. 70 For some, a slice is the easier shot . . .

If you find it easier to fade the ball, work on drawing it, just as Sam Snead did. Even players who hit fades all the time should practice hitting draws so that the fade doesn't become a slice. Great players, too. It doesn't take long for draws and fades to become hooks and slices. The late great English player Henry Cotton used to call these "contra-exercises." They are the most effective ways of keeping your swing "in the middle."

FIG. 71 for others, a hook is easier.

DRAWS BECOME HOOKS; FADES BECOME SLICES

That makes perfect sense and is something you should pay attention to. But if you're like most golfers your swing doesn't impart a gentle fade or draw on the ball. No, most of your shots are full-blown slices or hooks. Both have their drawbacks, not the least of which is that aiming is next to impossible because of the amount of curve you are putting on the ball.

A slice is a weak shot, the ball flying high and curving markedly from left-to-right. A hook, while undoubtedly more powerful, is even harder to control, the ball curving quickly from right-to-left.

Indeed, there are only two ways the golf ball can curve. Either you slice or you hook. Or at least you have a tendency to do one of the two. Probably at some point you have fought one and remnants remain in your golf swing. All golfers fall into at least one of those categories.

Everyone fights their natural tendency. You'll tend to aim and or swing in the opposite direction of your curvature mistake. And you'll tend to do things to compensate for the fact that your shots curve either to the left or the right.

Many people have a hard time either diagnosing or admitting that they slice or hook. Especially slicing. There seems to be a bit of social stigma attached to the slice. Some people even go as far as referring to it as a "push" or a "fade." But take it from me, everybody fights either a slice or a hook. Weaker players tend to have problems with a slice; stronger players with a hook.

Closely related to slices and hooks are pushes and pulls caused by the clubface. These are the most misdiagnosed shots in golf. The direction in which a shot starts out is a combination of the path of the swing—which accounts for only 25 percent—and the point of contact on the clubface (75 percent).

If the clubface is too closed or too open it is easy to pull or push the ball. The first stems from hitting the outside of the ball. Even though your swing path is straight through or to the right, you can still pull the ball to the left if the clubface is closed. If you hit a shot that starts left don't jump to the conclusion—like all the announcers do on television—that you came over the top and swung to the left. Check your divot. If it points to the left the problem was the path of your swing. If the divot is straight, the fault was in the clubface. Better players almost always pull with the clubface and not the path.

You can also hit a push if the face is wide open—by hitting the inside of the golf ball. If you hit a shot that starts off to the right it probably wasn't the path of your swing. The most common correction that is prescribed for a push is turning through more to finish the shot. But that isn't going to help. In fact, it will probably make things worse.

Even if you don't have much curvature on your ball, but you push or pull because of a misaligned clubface, we need to use the same corrections you would for a hook or a slice to fix those mistakes. Usually, any curvature shows up most with the driver. It is the straightest-faced club. And you hit more in the middle of the ball. All of which means that the driver will impart the most sidespin on the ball.

Look first at the plane of your swing coming into the ball. Too flat and you will tend to hook; too steep and you will tend to slice. If you are on plane and have a neutral grip and decent timing where your hands, arms, and body are working together, you are going to be able to hit pretty straight shots.

When your swing is too flat, the club comes into the ball too far inside and on a bigger arc, your hands tend to rotate very quickly through impact and you hook the ball. Those on too upright a plane tend to reverse-rotate their arms, block the face open, and slice the ball.

FIXING YOUR SLICE

As with all shots, you can trace the root cause of your slice. Fact one: The cause of a slice is that the clubface is open or opening through impact. Fact two: Slicers tend to swing too steeply. Fact three: What causes the face problem is usually the steep swing.

Slicing has nothing to do with cutting across the ball. An out-to-in swing path doesn't cause a slice. It never has caused a slice. It never will cause a slice. It is simply the characteristic of a slicer. Sure, it can aggravate a slice. But it doesn't cause it. For example, you can swing across the ball on an arc with the clubface closing and you'll hit a pull or a pull-hook, not a slice.

So your slice isn't caused by a path mistake. What comes first is the clubface being open. Most likely your swing is too steep coming into the ball and your arms are reverse-rotating to open the clubface. The clubhead is simply swinging off to the left to try and compensate for the open face. That ends up making the slice bigger.

So where do we start? With the clubface. We have to fix that. Make sure that your grip is strong enough. Make sure that your wrist position at the top isn't cupped—that opens the clubface and makes the swing more upright. Given those two factors, if you still slice your swing is almost certainly too steep. Or you are not squaring the back of your left hand at impact.

We need to get rid of that steepness, especially coming into the ball. Most people take the club inside on the backswing, lift it straight up, come down steep into the ball, and block the face open. That's one way to steepen the swing. Or the swing is too steep all the way through, up and down. Or you are taking the club back on a good plane and then steepening the downswing. Your problem has to be one of those.

When you are steep you have to find the source.

Is it the body? Turning the shoulders with too much of a tilting motion.

Is it the arm swing? Arms going straight up and down.

Is it taking the club away flat and lifting?

Is it a cupped left wrist at the top?

Or are your shoulders starting the downswing, causing the club to come down on too steep an arc? This can happen even after a good backswing.

The cause of your steepness is one of these.

Let's assume the club is moving too much inside on the takeaway (see fig. 72). That is the most common problem.

FIG. 72 Typically, a slicer takes the club away too much to the inside.

Is it happening because your hips, shoulders, and right side are pulling back too fast? That jerks the club to the inside so that you have to lift it up.

Are your arms pulling back too much or are your hands turning too quickly to the inside? All or any of those can cause you to lift the club to the top and then come down too steeply or "over the top."

Analyze, then try to reverse the loop. Get the club swinging back straighter and more up early in your swing. At least that is how it should feel. Your swing will still move the club to the inside of the ball target-line. But not inside and low. More up and inside.

Then let the club go around. So instead of in and up, you have the club moving up and around. The feeling will be that you are almost reversing the loop of your old swing. It's the same swing, but run in reverse. Instead of back flat and down steep, you are taking the club back a little steeper and down flatter.

The best way to practice this is with the club held a couple of feet

FIG. 73 Hold the club off the ground (a), make a "level" turn (b), then swing down (c) and up (d).

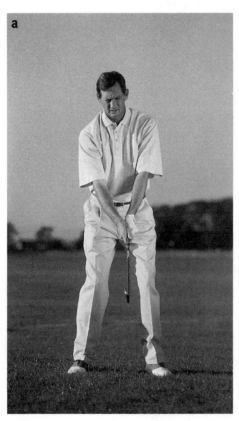

up off the ground (see figs. 73a, 73b, 73c, and 73d). Then make practice swings trying to swing the club on a consistent level plane in the backswing, one that is flatter than you would use in golf. When you swing the club down feel like your downswing is under the plane of your backswing—more to the right—and then up in the through swing. As you swing, feel your shoulders turning and your arms rotating. Feel the clubface opening and closing. The idea is that you practice this swing with the club off the ground and, as you go, lower the club down to the ground. The best clubs to use are the 5-iron and longer. A fairway wood is also good because it has more loft than a driver.

And, by the way, always tee the ball up when you are trying to fix an inside and over the top loop. Always. You'll find it easier to level out your steep approach into the ball.

If you get the clubhead swinging on that flatter plane, you are going to be able to square your hands through impact. There's no guarantee, of course, but it's easier. Focus on squaring the back of your

left hand at impact. In fact, if you are prone to big slices, try to square the clubface before impact. Take care though. You aren't trying to turn your hands over, but simply attempting to get the back of your left hand facing the target at impact.

Take a slightly stronger grip, one where the "Vs" formed by your thumbs and forefingers point more toward your right shoulder. You'll know you've gone too far if you start hooking. But before you panic, make sure you are hooking rather than pulling. If your ball starts to the right and truly hooks, back off toward a neutral grip again. The first goal is to get the ball hooking. Practice off a tee to start with. That will help shallow out your steep swing. Build success by clipping the ball off the tee.

If you start struggling with the ball on the ground, reverse the process. Tee the ball up, or go back to your practice swings with the club off the ground. There is no time frame. Take as long as you need. Go back to exaggerating the opposite feeling. Feel like you are making the opposite loop. And focus strongly on squaring the back of your left hand. This has to be a conscious thought if you slice.

Grip Pressure

You hear a lot about how all golfers should hold the club lightly, as if holding a bird (I don't know many people who hold birds—but I do know what they mean). And yes, it is great advice. Especially for those who slice. The tighter your hold on the club, the less active your hands will be in the swing and the more you will tend to block the release of your shots. A thinner grip can also help by encouraging more hand action through impact.

A larger circumference grip and a tighter pressure deactivates your hands in the swing. A softer grip pressure is always better for golfers who want to get their hands to work so that they can square the clubface at impact.

Too tight? Veins popping is too tight. Your grip pressure if you are trying to fix a slice should be softer than a manly handshake (see fig. 74). Much softer. Go with the dead fish handshake instead. For a hooker, about the same as a regular handshake is a good gauge.

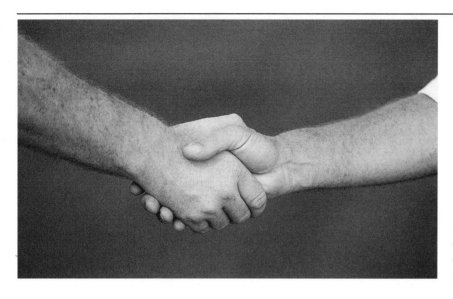

FIG. 74 To fix a slice, grip
the club much softer than
you would shake
someone's hand.

Timing

When you slice, the clubface is late in squaring up. Your body motion is often out ahead of the clubhead, so the face lags behind. Then you have to get everything squaring up earlier.

From the top of your backswing you want to feel like your right shoulder stays back and your hands and arms swing the club down. If your right shoulder jumps out into the shot, your club will subsequently come down steep and outside the plane. The steep approach will cause your arms to reverse rotate through the shot so the clubface will not square up at impact.

If you take the club back more up and around it is easier to keep your right shoulder back. A little adjustment to the stance can also help. Close it a little. Toe your left foot in a little, to the point where it is only just toed out. Toe the right foot out a little. You'll find it easier to turn on the backswing, much less so on the through swing.

FIXING YOUR HOOK

Very few people hook the ball. Quite a few hit some pulls and think they hook the ball, but few fight a shot which starts off to the right and finishes to the left. Hooking the ball is definitely a better player's mistake. In fact, it is true to say that every great ball-striker in the history of the game has fought a hook at one time or another. Those who hook the ball do so for one of these reasons:

1. They move the club and their hands and arms too quickly relative to the body. Thus, the clubface squares up too early and is closed by the time impact occurs.
2. They swing the club on too flat a plane so that the club comes into the ball either too much from the inside or behind them (see figs. 75a and 75b). This means the club is swinging on too much of an arc and leads to the clubface turning over too much through the shot.
3. Their grips are too strong or otherwise faulty.

I always tell my students that if there is a road to good golf, nowhere on that road is there a slice. You can go from hooking to

FIG. 75a,b Better players who hook tend to leave the club too far behind them on the downswing (a). Ideally, the club should be more out in front of you (b).

a No

b Yes

good golf. You can go from slicing to hooking to good golf. But you can't go from slicing to good golf. So a hook isn't all bad. Here's how to fix one.

The Grip

The first thing to check is your grip. Look for a couple of things. Are your hands close together? If not, move them closer.

Keep constant pressure with your right hand on your left thumb. There must be no looseness there. That can cause your hands to grab the club and close the face somewhere in the swing.

Checkpoint One

The "Vs" of your thumbs and forefingers should be pointing toward your right cheekbone (see fig. 75c). That's a neutral grip.

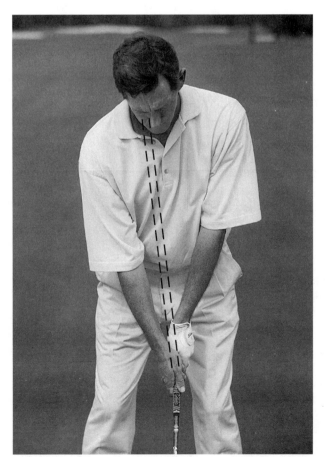

FIG. 75c In a neutral grip, your "Vs" should point toward your right cheek.

Checkpoint Two

At the top you want the clubface in a neutral position where the clubface is at the same angle as the clubshaft was at address. Somewhere in between the toe pointing to the ground and the clubface facing the sky. Check yours in a mirror. If the face is looking skyward, the clubface is closed. Check again to make sure your grip is neutral. You don't want to have the club turning in your hands as you swing back. And be sure that your left wrist is flat and not bowed at the top of your swing. A bowed left wrist will close the clubface.

Timing

Does your hook stem from your inability to get your body turning through along with your hands and arms? If your body isn't moving, you are going to tend to hook the ball. Feel like your body and hips are turning through faster. That will improve your timing.

The Classic Better Player's Mistake

The mistake I see in most players fighting a hook is that the club is stuck behind them with the club swinging into the ball on too flat of a swing plane or too far from the inside. This is a classic better player's mistake. A relatively poor player gets the club more out in front of him and has the club coming into the ball at a much steeper angle.

But the better player tends to get the club moving on too flat an arc and leaves it behind him. Typically he has fought a hook and is now trying not to go left. So he drops the club inside to keep the club from crossing over. Of course, when that happens, it crosses over even more.

Fix that mistake by getting the club on plane going back. An upright shaft in the backswing will always tend to flatten too much in the downswing, especially if you are a better than average player. Swing back on your original shaft angle. Rotate your left forearm to get the club on plane as it moves up. The rotation allows you to make the opposite move on the downswing, rotating your left arm down and into your side. That gets the clubhead out in front of you and the clubshaft on the correct swing plane.

In the backswing you want to make sure that you keep your hands and arms out in front of your body. If your arms swing past your turn in the backswing, the club will get stuck behind you at the start of the downswing. Then, as you move into the downswing, your shoulders will start to turn through before your hands and arms start down. If the shoulders go first a better player will leave the club behind; this will lead to the club coming into the ball too much from the inside and behind you. From that position you have two choices. Stay back and hit a hook. Or turn on top of the shot with your right shoulder and block the ball straight right.

From the top there should also be a feeling of your hips moving laterally. Your weight should shift from your right heel to your left big toe right as you start the downswing. And your shoulders must stay back if you are going to rotate your left arm and get the club out in front of you. All of which encourages you to hit the inside part of ball.

This hooking business is a tough mistake, especially when your instincts are to drop the club inside and hang back to keep the ball from hooking. Of course, those are exactly the reasons why a ball hooks. So it is a vicious circle. Golf is very much a game of opposites. So correcting your ball-flight pattern can often mean fighting your basic instincts.

Part Three

Using Your Swing

7

What Every Golfer Wants
Twenty More Yards

There is a very simple reason why the longest hitters in golf have always drawn the biggest crowds. Watching and striking long drives may be the most fun in the game. Distance is a thrill, as all the "oohs" and "aahs" you hear after Tiger Woods, John Daly, or Laura Davies uncork a really big drive testify. Even if they can't reproduce the same shot themselves, people love to watch a long ball soar away into the distance.

Which is fine. But there is another side to the coin. If you have read any of the more pompous instruction books you'll no doubt have been told that distance does not necessarily translate into low scores. If you really want to get better at golf, say the know-it-alls, you should work instead on your short-game. Get out there and whack some chips. Slam dunk those putts. Sounds like fun, right? Wrong.

While there is no disputing the benefits of a polished short-game when it comes to adding up your score at the end of eighteen holes, it isn't what I see people practicing. All I see at any of my own facilities is hundreds of people hitting balls and a handful of people chipping and putting. That tells me something. Even though everyone knows that the short-game is the route to better scores, it isn't what most people want to work on.

Golfers play the game for a variety of reasons. Some like the exercise. Some like the camaraderie at the club. Many like the competitive aspect. Just as many want to shoot the lowest number they can every time out. But most people simply like to hit the ball well and far; the score is secondary.

That's why this chapter is in this book. Who am I to tell you how to have fun?

DRILLS

At this point I'd like to mention why there are no so-called "drills" in this chapter or, indeed, this book. You know the sort of thing I mean. Beach balls between your legs. Straps under your arms. Hitting one-handed or off one leg.

Drills became popular with teachers at golf schools. They are fine in that environment, where everyone is "trapped" for a period of time and has no option but to practice. But, individually, I've never seen anyone do even one. People don't do drills. Even if, over the last few years, golfers have been conditioned to expect them in books and magazines.

So prescribing drills for you is a waste of time. Drills aren't fun. Fun is hitting balls and hitting better shots. If you're like most golfers, you don't want to stand out on the range looking ridiculous, which is how you'll appear wearing some of the goofy apparatus I see on the market nowadays.

Besides, drills aren't very effective. To get anything from a drill you really need supervision. They are easy to mess up and they exist mostly as second-rate replacements for a teacher. Actually, that's not quite true. Those training aids also exist so that the teacher endorsing them can make more money.

So what's the alternative? People need to know what they should be thinking and feeling during the swing. They need to know what their swings look like. And you can capture all three in front of a mirror.

And that's what I want you to do. If you have an hour to work on your game, spend at least five minutes in front of a mirror. You have to have a picture in your mind and a feel for whatever it is we're talking about in this book (which is what the photographs are for).

A real key to improving your swing—once you have a picture of what you are trying to do—is developing a good practice swing. By good I mean correct. Most golfers think they have a good practice swing because it is slow and smooth. But that isn't enough. Your practice swing also has to incorporate correct body motion and have the club on plane. When you can produce that sort of practice swing, hit some balls and see how it works for real. My bet is you'll see an immediate improvement.

DISTANCE

There are two elements necessary to playing good golf—distance and direction. Distance is a very important aspect of the game. To a great extent it determines your potential in golf.

Distance can also give you accuracy. The longer you hit the ball from the tee, the closer you will finish to the green. That means you'll be hitting more lofted clubs for your approach shots. You'll hit the putting surface more often with a 7-iron than you will with a 5-iron. So more distance will help you in areas other than in pure yardage.

Plus, good distance allows you to avoid using your driver every time up. If you hit the ball long enough, you can go to your 3-wood or a long iron from the tee. In the long run you'll hit more fairways that way. As we've covered already, the greater loft on the 3-wood creates more backspin, which negates sidespin, and lets you hit straighter shots. Even with a slightly unorthodox swing.

YOU CAN DO IT

The great thing about golf is that you can hit a shot as well as the best player in the world, but you'll never hit a drive as far as Tiger Woods can. It just won't happen. But everyone can hit it farther than they do now.

I have yet to meet the golfer who hits the ball as far as he can on a consistent basis. Even Tiger Woods. Everything he does in his swing is designed to increase his control, not his distance. He makes only a three-quarter backswing and plays most of his shots at less than full speed. There are a few things he could do to hit the ball longer. But he doesn't need that.

Control comes from having a good golf swing or lack of distance. If you don't hit your shots very far they won't go very far off-line. But distance comes from having a good, powerful, fast swing. Some of that is God-given, but there are some things you can do to get maybe twenty extra yards. You can hook the ball. You can improve your approach into the ball. Too steep an approach wastes clubhead speed. You can create a bigger arc, or more turn, or more wrist cock, and you can probably unleash some of the speed you aren't using.

CAN DISTANCE BE BOUGHT?

The short answer is yes; a qualified yes. Every equipment company promises you more distance through longer drivers. And, for once, they are right. The standard length for a driver used to be forty-three inches. Now it is forty-five to forty-six inches. Shaft length is really the only way to buy distance. You have to earn everything else. Automatically you have a bigger arc, even if you don't do anything different.

Even if you don't cock your wrists any more. Even if you don't turn any more. Even if you don't swing your arms any further back. With a longer shaft in your driver you can have a bigger arc, which automatically translates into more clubhead speed. That's why bigger, taller players, those with longer arms, can potentially hit the ball farther than a more diminutive player.

SWING FASTER—NOT SLOWER

All is not lost even if you aren't exactly the Arnold Schwarzenegger of golf. If you are short, but very quick, you can still hit it out there with a big, slower-swinging player. The speed of your swing is vital in producing distance. Most people swing the club too slow. Most people hit hard, not fast. You want to hit fast; as fast as possible. Yet all too often I hear people complaining that they swing too fast! They come for lessons and tell me they swing too fast. Then I ask them what their goals are and they tell me they want to hit the ball farther! If you want to find your maximum distance then first you need to find your maximum swing speed.

That's why all long hitters have fast swings. They may not look fast in that some have a lazy rhythm, but all create enormous clubhead speed through impact. When I was teaching at Pinehurst Hotel & Country Club a young University of North Carolina student by the name of Davis Love III used to come there to practice. One day I saw him on the swing speed machine. He would routinely clock 135 mph. When he tried to pick up the pace he could do 145 mph. That's the clubhead speed of Tiger Woods and John Daly. Davis has since toned his speed down but he has that capability. Fred Couples is very fast, too.

The average player swings around 85 mph, yet he thinks he is swinging too fast. There is a difference between hitting hard with your body and hitting fast with your hands. Believe me, you want to pick up the pace of your swing. Every golfer could probably squeeze a few miles per hour out of his swing. Every mph is worth about 2.5 yards. So 10 yards more means 4 mph faster. That may not sound like much, but it is a lot. It's hard to find 4 mph, but you can do it. Especially if you have been trying to swing slowly!

Work on making your whole swing faster. That old adage about "slow back" is nonsense. You need a consistent, smoothly accelerating tempo—slow back, down fast is too jerky—to hit the ball farther and still be able to find it.

LOFT

This is a common mistake. All the time I see people with "powerful" drivers, those with only six and a half or seven degrees loft. They think they are buying distance with these clubs. But they're not. Those straight-faced clubs are actually more difficult to hit. Sure, your one-in-a-hundred best hit might go a long way, but you'll never be consistent. In truth, all you're really buying is more slice.

A BIGGER TURN

Okay, you're going for the big one. As with most things in life, there is a right way and a wrong way. The wrong way is a muscle-bulging, eye-popping slash at the ball which almost throws you off your feet. Instead, you need to channel what strength you have in the proper directions. Here's how.

First, take a little wider stance. Turn out your right foot (see fig. 76). That will help you turn more on the backswing, which allows you to swing down into the back of ball. A square hit is essential; a glancing blow between club and ball is a waste of clubhead speed and, ultimately, yardage.

Once set up, focus on turning your shoulders more, and cocking your wrists more. But more than anything, focus on your hands and arms. Getting them to work properly allows you to really pick up the pace of your swing.

The idea that you can get more out of it by moving your body faster makes little sense. A faster body can be a slight multiplier of speed, but it doesn't create the speed. Body swingers struggle for distance. Nick Faldo is a classic example. Using your body more doesn't

FIG. 76 For more distance, widen your stance and turn your right foot out more.

give you more distance; it gives you more accuracy. Because it quiets your hands. Whenever you do that you give up distance.

The faster your hands are, the more you can square them quickly at the ball. Then the later you can wait to square the clubface. If your hands are slow you have to release earlier so that you can be sure to have the clubface square at impact.

The quicker your hands are, the more you can delay the hit. The more you delay the hit, the more powerful you can become. You snap your release right at the bottom of the shot. Now, that's a dangerous thought for those of you who slice. Yes, you can get more distance, but first you must get the ball to hook. You can't try to delay the hit unless you already have the ball drawing. If a slicer tries to delay the hit, he will slice even more than usual.

Especially if the fairways are firm and dry, a drive shaped from right-to-left will run more on landing. Anyone fading the ball is losing distance compared to one who is hitting a draw.

To get a draw you need the proper angle of approach into the ball. That is key. If you take X amount of clubhead speed and you put it at too steep of an angle into impact, you're wasting your power into the ground instead of using it to smack the back of the ball.

Your adjustments start at address. First, close your stance a little by pulling your right foot back from square and aligning the rest of your body parallel to your feet (see fig. 77). Also turn your right foot out a bit more than usual. That will encourage you to turn more in the backswing. And don't worry. None of that will knock you off plane; all you have done is tilt your plane to the right. Which makes sense. You want the ball to start right and curve left.

Move the ball back in your stance a little bit. Exactly how much depends on how big a curve you want to hit. The more right-to-left shape you want, the more you have to move the ball back. These adjustments to your alignment shift the point at which the bottom of your swing occurs. In this case, back of where it would normally be. Moving the ball back compensates for that.

Looking down at the club behind the ball, it should appear slightly open to the ball-target line. That sends you the message that you want the clubface to be closing—not closed—as you contact the ball. You want the clubface aligned where you want the ball to start.

This setup will encourage the club to swing back into the ball, more from the inside. All of which gives your hands more time to release through the shot. The more hand action you employ, the more right-to-left spin you impart on the ball.

Start slowly. Don't try to hit the ball too hard at first. Focus on your hands and the clubface. Feel how the knuckles of your left hand turn all the way down to face the ground, closing the clubface as it moves through impact and beyond.

FIG. 77 Closing your stance will help you hit a draw.

"SWISH"

This will also help you focus on your hands and arms. When you take a practice swing, hold the club up off the ground and listen for your "swish." The louder your swish, the farther you will hit the golf ball.

Provided you square the clubface up. If you make a real loud swish but the clubface is wide open, you'll hit a big slice to the right. As we've seen, that's the way to lose, not gain, distance.

8

Pitching the Ball Into the Air and Greenside Bunker Play

There are three shots you know you are always going to get in any round of golf. Unless you want to be short at every long par-4, you will have to use your driver sometime. Everyone has to putt, of course. And everyone has to pitch the ball in the air.

Pitching the ball in the air is one of the essentials for playing golf well. No matter what, during the course of eighteen holes you are going to be stuck with a water hazard or a bunker or some kind of obstacle in front of you. So you can't avoid having to pitch the golf ball high enough to carry over trouble and onto the green. It's just something you have to be able to do.

If you don't believe me, consider this. In any eighteen-hole round the average player will three-putt maybe two or three times. He'll likely incur a penalty shot, perhaps two. He'll somehow scrape together four or five pars. He'll hit around five or six greens on a good day.

That last statistic is the important one, at least as far as pitching is concerned. If our average guy hits five or six greens that means he must miss at least twelve. Of those, maybe four times he can chip his ball onto the putting surface. Which leaves eight pitch shots. Other than driving or putting, that makes pitching the most important shot in your bag.

WHAT IS A PITCH?

The short game consists of putting, chipping, and pitching. Whenever you can, you want to putt. Whenever you can't putt, you chip, keeping the ball as close to the ground as possible. And whenever you can't chip, you pitch.

A pitch shot is used whenever a chip shot won't get over an obstacle or stop quickly enough to finish close to the hole. There are a few ways to define a pitch shot. I prefer this one. A pitch shot is generally a short shot played from turf with a sand wedge. In a typical pitch, the ball spends maybe 90 percent of its time in the air, 10 percent on the ground.

A pitch can be anything from five yards up to anything less than a full swing with a sand wedge. If you hit your sand wedge a maximum of, say, seventy yards, anything less is a pitch. It's a partial shot, which is one of the things which makes it tricky to play consistently well.

WHY I LIKE PITCHING

A pitch shot swing is really just a full swing in miniature. In effect, it is the beginning of your full swing. Golfers who improve their pitching also improve their takeaways. And since the golf swing is a building process, the better you do at the beginning, the better your swing will be in the middle, at the top, and coming down. You build your swing right from the start.

Golfers who have mistakes in their swing typically make the same errors with all clubs. The same with the takeaway. If you take your driver away low and inside, the face shut, you'll do the same with a wedge. But the opposite is also true. If you can fix your takeaway with the wedge, doing the same with the driver should be easier. That way, all the clubs and all your swings have a consistency to them. You won't be pitching with one style and driving with another. You have the same takeaway for all. More on that later.

So hitting pitch shots is a way for you to practice your full swing. It's also an easy way to practice. Hitting pitch shots doesn't require much energy. You can only hit so many drives in a day before you get worn out. And once you get tired, hitting too many balls is counterproductive anyway. Besides, it is always good if you have some extra short game practice. Pitching is also a good place to start your pre-round warm-up.

Good pitching builds confidence. If you can pitch the ball well, you will worry less about missing the green and consequently make better full swings. When you play with fear, trying not to hit it, say, where you have to pitch over a sand trap, invariably that's right where you go. And the opposite is true. The less you worry about hitting your ball in a tough spot, the less often you will find yourself with a hazard to pitch over.

That's why I like pitching and why I think it is so important.

HOW TO PITCH

The Setup

Pitching technique and sand technique are not much different. A sand shot is usually just a little bigger pitch shot swing. When I think of practicing pitching, I'm thinking of a shot that is 10–15 yards long. You expand that swing to hit a longer pitch, up to a three-quarters swing. Which is basically the same as a sand shot. The only real difference is that, in a bunker, the sand offers more resistance to the club. So you need to make a bigger, faster swing.

Vary the distance you hit your pitch shots by varying two things: the length of the swing you make—on both sides of ball— and how much the clubface is open. Pitch with a slightly open clubface as a minimum.

Strangely, you never pitch the ball with a pitching wedge. That club is misnamed. You use it to hit a full shot with, or to chip with. But never to hit a pitch with. Maybe you would use it to hit a long "pitch and run" in somewhere like Scotland, where the ground is hard and it is generally windy, but you can argue that is more of a long chip.

Anyway, a true pitch is played with a sand wedge (see fig. 78). On that club the leading edge is the digging part of the club and the bot-

FIG. 78 The flange on a sand wedge helps the club glide through impact.

tom or the flange is the bouncing or gliding part of the club. If you play a pitch shot with the clubface square, you won't hit the ball as high and your tendency will be to dig into the ground a little bit.

So lay the face open, just as you do in a sand trap (see fig. 79). Then take your grip. That allows the club to slide under the ball, adding loft to the shot. Don't get fearful looking down at the open face, imagining you will hit the ball off to the right. The reality is that the more you set the face open, the more you hit underneath the ball. Your contact point might be just a little bit to the inside of the ball, but it is mostly underneath the ball, sending it up into the air.

You also open your body, of course. And your swing is more to the left than a full swing would be (see figs. 80a and 80b). When you set up with an open clubface to the right, open your body to the left to compensate. They should match up.

Like the clubface, your body should always be at least a little open. You're only making a short swing, so you want room for your arms to pass by your body. You need freedom to get the club through the shot and your body out of the way and a slightly open stance definitely helps this. For those reasons, and to help you get the ball in the air, place the ball more forward in your stance. Your weight should be evenly distributed.

FIG. 79 Open the clubface at address, just as you would in a bunker.

FIG. 80 Open your stance at least a little for all pitch shots (a)

. . . then swing to the left (b).

THE SWING

Any momentum is created primarily with your arms, but also with some wrist cock. A pitch shot is a sweeping motion. You don't want to take too much divot. Let the club slide under the ball.

Poor pitchers tend to use their hands too much in an attempt to lift the ball into the air. Forget that. The loft on the club will provide the elevation you need.

The one staple in the swing is that your arms swing back and forth. The amount of body turn should match the amount of your arm swing. You turn your shoulders back, your lower body through, while your arms swing back and forth. Start your swing along the line of your shoulders. Not your toes. Your shoulders are generally less open than your feet. Only when playing a real high lob shot should you open your shoulders as much as your feet. Then you should swing along the line of your toes.

When you swing the club back, the most important point is where the shaft is parallel to the ground and the target-line. At that stage the club should be in a "toe-up" position (see fig. 81).

Your right wrist should be relatively flat (see figs. 82a and 82b), not bent back (the more you bend it back, the more the club gets behind you and the more you tend to get the face closed. Then the leading edge digs into the ground). Then all you have to do is let your club brush the ground.

That is the main difference between a full swing and a pitch swing–the fact that you have the face open at least slightly at address and keep it open throughout the swing. Having said that, it doesn't hurt to have the clubface too open. Players who have the face open usually pitch well, those with the face shut have a hard time.

People who have trouble pitching also usually have something wrong with the beginning of their swing. The beginning of your full swing is really your pitch shot. With a full swing you have a chance to correct early mistakes. With a pitch shot you don't have the time to do that. Someone with a bad takeaway can still hit a good drive,

FIG. 81 When the shaft is close to horizontal, the clubface should be "toe up."

FIG. 82 Keep the back of your right wrist close to flat (a). Bend it too much and the club moves too far behind you, the face closed (b).

but can't hit too many good pitches because he doesn't get to the point of his correction in such a little swing. That's why a pitch shot will tell you much about the early part of your swing.

Trajectory

When you want to hit the ball higher, widen your stance, bend from your knees and hips a little more, and stand further from the ball to lower your center of gravity (see figs. 83a and 83b). Those changes will also have the effect of lowering your hands at address. You lower your hands when you want to hit the ball higher. The lower your hands are, the more effective loft there will be on the club.

Here's what not to do. Don't choke down on the club. Hold it normally. The more you choke down on the club, the closer you get to the ball. The closer you get to the ball the more upright the shaft is. An upright shaft only serves to reduce the effective loft on the club.

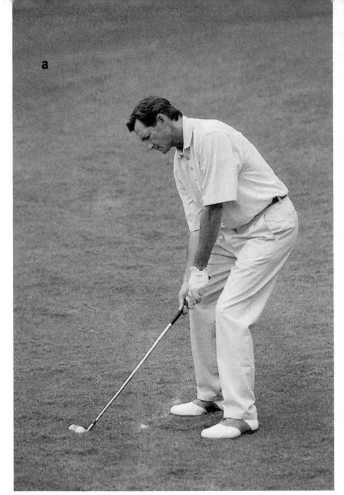

FIG. 83 To pitch the ball high in the air, widen your stance, move back, and lower your hands (a). Then slide the clubhead under the ball (b).

And don't forget. As soon as you lower your hands and increase the loft on the club you are going to have to increase the speed and length of your swing in order to achieve the same distance you would if your hands were higher and the loft less.

Tough Lies

If the lie is really bare, pitching is difficult. You have so little margin for error. The bottom of your swing must be right at the ball. With the clubface open, the flange on the club will tend to make it bounce off hard pan and up into the belly of the ball, even if you hit only a little behind the shot.

The solution? Lean toward more of a chip shot. Literally. Ease more weight into your left side at address. And play the ball back a bit further in your stance with the clubface only slightly open at address. You'll find it easier to contact the ball and the ground at the same time. But don't have high expectations. Even the best players in the world need some grass under the ball if they are going to hit effective and consistent pitch shots.

In fact, if the lie is really severe, don't even consider playing a pitch shot. Chip, even if it means playing away from the flag. A thirty-foot putt is better than a chunked or bladed pitch.

SAND

If you're like most golfers, you're not thrilled when your ball ends up in a sand trap. "I just can't get the ball out of there," is a phrase I've heard any number of times over the years. The root cause, of course, is poor technique. But long-term failure that leads to a negative attitude is also there. That only exacerbates any technical problems.

The saddest part is that, as I'm sure you've heard a million times, bunker play needn't be the scariest aspect of golf. With a sound method you should be able to routinely escape the sand in less than two shots. Here's how.

The Basics

On a standard greenside bunker shot the clubhead shouldn't actually make contact with the ball. Instead, you want to hit underneath the ball. The sand carries the ball out of the trap. So even though you are playing a kind of a pitch shot swing, you need to adjust your setup a little.

As with the pitch shot, the clubface must be open for a bunker shot, if only a little for some shots. Vary the "V" that is formed by your clubface aiming right and your body left depending on the length and height of the shot you want to hit. A longish shot has a narrow "V," a short shot has a wide "V." (see figs. 84a and 84b)

The difference is that when you set up, the ball has to be more forward in your stance than it was for a pitch (see fig. 85). Remember, you are not going to hit the ball, just the sand. In fact, an error in ball position is the most common mistake I see. People set up square with the ball in the middle of their stances. Almost always I am suggesting that my students open up a little more and put the ball farther forward.

FIG. 84 Short sand shot—open your stance and clubface to make a wide V (a). Long sand shot—less open to narrow the V (b).

FIG. 85 Move the ball forward in your stance for a basic sand shot.

So that you don't slip, dig your feet into the sand. That lowers your center of gravity, which makes it easier for you to hit underneath the ball.

Another common error I see: Don't grip down unless the sand is very soft and your feet are sinking more than an inch. It is the digging of your feet into the sand which allows you to slide the clubhead under the ball. Assuming the sand is neither too soft nor too hard (more on both later) you only want to hit an inch under the ball.

As for your grip, hold on a little tighter than you would normally. It's as if you are playing from deep rough. You need the clubface to stay open and face skyward through impact. A soft grip will tend to make the clubface close when it hits the sand.

The Swing

Again, as in a pitch shot, use the beginning of your full swing (see fig. 86). But make a bigger swing than you would with a pitch shot. Almost every sand shot is at least a three-quarter swing. Even on a really short shot you should simply make a slower swing.

How far behind the ball you want to contact the sand is another great point of debate in golf. Why, I don't know. For me it isn't such

FIG. 86 Use your normal takeaway along the line of your feet for a sand shot.

a big deal. You just don't have to be that precise. Ideal may be half an inch behind the ball, but there is a big margin for error. Four to six inches behind with a fast enough swing and a full follow-through will get the ball out of the bunker and onto the green.

Besides, the last thing you want to do is put pressure on yourself to be perfect. Consider that the best players in the world get up and down in two shots from greenside bunkers only about 60 percent of the time. So if you get out in one shot and two-putt, you're not far behind the best in the world. That's plenty good enough for most people who play golf.

Hard/Soft Sand

Unfortunately, in the real world, the ball doesn't always find the middle of the bunker. And, more importantly, the texture of the sand can change from course to course and even from hole to hole. Hard-packed sand and soft, deep sand offer two very different challenges.

All of which means, as you'd expect, some adjustments to your basic technique depending on how much sand is under the ball. Once you add the following variations to your sand play, you'll never think of bunkers with a sense of dread again.

Setup Dictates Swing Shape

Whenever the sand beneath your ball is hard or wet or both, chances are you aren't going to be able to hit down very much. It'll be too tough for the club to dig into the sand to any great extent. So you can hit down as much as you want to, as long as the clubhead hits the sand close to the ball.

To get that job done, you need a swing that is abruptly "V" shaped. You have to swing the club up and down fairly steeply. Think "up and down" (see figs. 87a, 87b, 87c, and 87d).

There's much you can do to encourage that ideal. Open the clubface only slightly at address. You want more of the sharper leading edge in this shot so that the club can get "into" the sand. You want more "dig" than "bounce." This is the same basic technique you should use when the ball is buried or plugged in the sand. The more you need the club to dig the ball out, the more square you need to make the clubface.

Three more things. Your stance should follow the lead of the clubface in that it should be only very slightly open. Lower your hands at

FIG. 87 When the sand is hard (a), pick the club and your arms up steeply (b, c), then hit down behind the ball (d).

address. They should sit just above the level of your knees. And place a little more weight on your left side. All will encourage the "up and down" motion you need.

Think "Up," Then "Down"

Into the backswing, start to cock your wrists early and swing your arms on a more up and down swing plane. When your hands are waist high, the clubhead should already be even with your chin. And when your hands reach hip height, your wrists should be fully cocked, the clubshaft close to vertical. That's the "up" part.

In contrast, think "down" through impact. Really go for it. Stick the club in the sand and keep going into an abbreviated follow-through.

More Room for Soft Sand

The swing shape you are looking for here is more of a "U" than a "V." You want the clubhead to slide through the sand rather than plough into it. You want more "bounce" than "dig."

Again, most of your adjustments are made at address. This time open the clubface so that the flange on the back of the head is the first part of the club to contact the sand. That will encourage the club to skim through the sand, sending a small scoop of sand—and the ball—onto the green.

Your stance should be open to the target line, your feet dug well into the sand. You need a firm base for this shot. Remember, if your feet dig more than an inch into the sand, you need to choke down on the club an equal amount so that the clubhead doesn't hit too far under the ball (see figs. 88a, 88b, 88c, and 88d).

Slide the Clubhead

The swing you want to make here is much wider than the one you make for firm sand. The fact that your hands are higher, you are standing taller, and your weight is evenly balanced will all encourage that width.

On the backswing there is much less need for wrist cock. When your hands are waist high the clubhead should be only a little higher. Replace that "up" move with more extension in your backswing to promote a slightly shallower approach.

FIG. 88 When the sand is soft (a), make a wide, U-shaped swing (b, c), then slide the clubhead under the ball (d).

Coming down, think of your move through impact as cutting a slice of sand from the bunker. And make sure to finish your swing. Keep the clubhead going, all the way into a fullish follow-through.

SOME DO'S AND DON'TS

While it is important that you know how to play from all types of sand and lies, there are—as in every part of golf—some constants in bunker technique. Here are a few do's and don'ts to keep in mind.

At Address

FIG. 89 The clubface should be a little open for a sand shot . . .

FIG. 90 or really open . . .

FIG. 91 but never square.

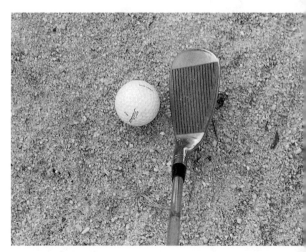

FIG. 92 The ball should be opposite your left heel for a sand shot . . .

FIG. 93 or a couple of inches back . . .

FIG. 94 but never back of center.

On the Backswing

FIG. 95 The club should move back along your toe-line . . .

FIG. 96 or outside that line . . .

FIG. 97 but never inside.

Impact

FIG. 98 The club should hit the sand six inches behind the ball . . .

FIG. 99 or three inches behind the ball . . .

FIG. 100 . . . or an inch behind the ball.

But never at the ball.

Follow-Through

FIG. 101 Your hands should finish head high on basic sand shot . . .

FIG. 102 or waist high . . .

FIG. 103 but never lower
than that.

9

Short Shots
Putting and Chipping

PUTTING

Putting represents the sharp end of golf. Good putting can cover up a multitude of ball-striking sins and make a bad score okay, an okay score good, and a good score great. Bad putting, on the other hand, can do just the opposite. There is nothing more frustrating than hitting a string of good drives and approach shots, then missing every putt.

Putting, then, is a game within a game. The fact that you have a sound, on-plane full swing means nothing when you get on the greens. Good putting requires a whole different technique. And this makes sense when you think about it. Uniquely in golf, a well-struck putt stays on the ground all the time. And to achieve that you really don't want to move your body at all. A good stroke is one where you swing the club with your arms and shoulders. Every other swing involves at least a little body movement to get you through the shot with some rhythm and timing.

Still, in putting there are more ways of getting the job done effectively than in any other part of golf. The relative shortness of the stroke allows you much more flexibility in terms of method. Indeed, putting is a test of feel, touch, and nerve as much as technique. If you don't have those first three qualities, it really doesn't matter how good your stroke is. That is why you can make putts using a variety of putting grips, many more screwy-looking setups, and certainly a lot of different putters.

Having said that, there are two distinct putting styles used by the vast majority of golfers. There is the open-to-closed "swinging gate" method used by, among others, Ben Crenshaw. Then there is the more straight-back, straight-through stroke. The vast majority of players on the professional tours favor that approach. And I must admit I share their preference. I like straight back–straight through, the face square to the line from start to finish. It's simpler. But each method has its own distinct characteristics.

Open-to-Closed

From address to the end of the follow-through the putter stays close to the ground. The putter face opens on the backswing, then closes on the through swing. In that respect it is almost like a miniature full swing, although the arc it follows is, of course, flat.

Generally, this stroke is long and flowing. You need good tempo to make it work effectively. There should be a smooth, rather than easily discernible, acceleration of the blade through impact. For that reason, open-to-closed putters are usually above average lag putters.

As you'd expect, because the face of the club is square to the target for only a short length of time, the position of the ball within the stance is crucial. There is no margin for error as far as moving the ball forward or back is concerned. Too far back and you will tend to push the putt to the right; too far forward and you will tend to pull the ball to the left.

You'll probably feel more comfortable with a fairly upright posture, your arms hanging almost straight down. That makes it easy for you to make the stroke with your arms and shoulders. There should be virtually no wrist action.

If you favor this style of putting, you will find it easier to achieve with a heel-shafted putter. It will allow you to stand tall and away from the ball. The clubface rotates around the shaft, accommodating the open-to-closed shape of the stroke.

Straight Back–Straight Through

This method typically involves a shorter and more "up-down-up" type of stroke (see figs. 104a, 104b, and 104c). That gives you more leniency in terms of where the ball should be within your feet. Really, it can be anywhere from opposite your left big toe if your left eye is set up over the ball, to the center of your stance if your head is set up behind the ball.

Where there must be no doubt is in how far you stand from the ball. It is a great advantage if your eye-line is directly over the target-

FIG. 104
Think "up a little (a) . . .
down a little (b) . . .
up a little" (c).

line. In fact, this is the only shot in golf where it is possible for you to look directly down the target-line. To achieve that you will probably have to bend over more from the waist.

Move the putter back and forth by rocking your shoulders, straight back and straight through. There should be no feeling of the clubhead moving inside or outside the target-line at any point during the stroke.

Use a center-shafted or face-balanced putter for this method. Having the shaft more toward the middle of the blade gets your head more over the ball, and encourages the straightness you want in your stroke and the squareness you want in the putter-face.

Take note, however. On really long putts, no matter what your technique, you are going to have a stroke that has some arc to it. Eventually, the clubhead just has to move inside the line. But as far as your thoughts and feelings are concerned, change nothing. Just let it happen.

Loft

Whatever putting style you end up favoring, don't forget the importance of loft on your putter. Yes, loft. Believe it or not, putters generally have anywhere from three to seven degrees of loft. Depending on the greens or your style of putting, you might need a putter with a different amount of loft. In general, the tighter the greens are cut, the less loft you want. The shaggier or grainier the greens are, the more loft you want. More loft helps you get the ball rolling on top of the grass.

Factor in your putting style. Maybe you like your hands farther forward at address. If so, you need more loft. You are, in effect, de-lofting the club with this hand position. If you like your hands back more, you want less loft on your putter.

Arms and Shoulders

Again, this is my preference. I like to see my pupils putting with the arms and shoulders. I like to see them maintain the triangle formed by their arms and shoulders from address to post-impact. That is the technique employed by most of the best putters on tour. But there are other ways. Billy Casper, one of the greatest putters ever, had a very wristy, "pop" type stroke. So I can't in all honesty say that using your hands in the stroke is necessarily wrong.

But less hands is better if you're struggling. Also, always make sure your wrists are in a relaxed position and not arched up at address or during your stroke (see figs. 105a and 105b). If that happens it is difficult to keep a consistent stroke where the face and path stays square throughout the stroke.

The Grip

Most professionals use the reverse overlap grip for putting (see figs. 106a and 106b). The idea is that it helps eliminate wrist action from the stroke. In it, the forefinger of your left hand overlaps the little finger of your right hand. Or the forefinger extends down over all four fingers. That tends to keep your hands out of the stroke and keep your wrists firm, which is what I advocate on putting.

While it is a personal thing, I like to see both thumbs going straight down the shaft. And both palms facing and perpendicular to the target-line. But, again, you can hold the club any way you want to within reason. If it works, of course!

FIG. 105 Your wrists should be relaxed when you address a putt (a), not arched (b).

a **Yes**

b **No**

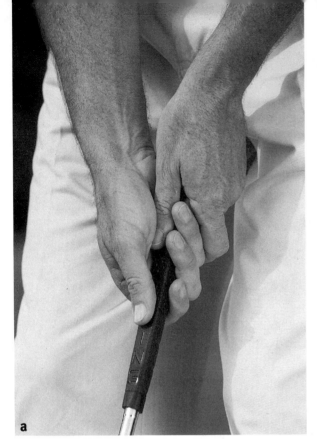
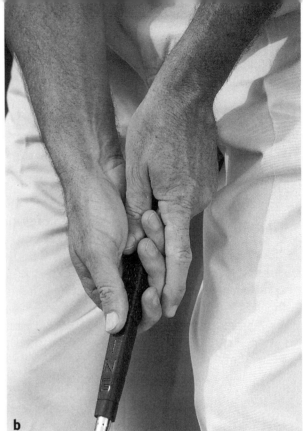

FIG. 106 In a reverse overlap putting grip, your left forefinger can overlap (a) or extend (b).

Distance

How far you hit your putts is a much underrated aspect of putting. No one seems to pay much attention to distance-control, so it's no surprise that it is the biggest weakness I see in amateurs.

Realize that if you don't hit every putt solid, your feel will constantly have to adjust to the vagaries of your stroke. For example, if you hit the ball off the toe of the putter it won't go far enough. Do that long enough and frustration inevitably sets in. So all of a sudden you hit the next putt harder and catch it solid—and it runs ten feet past. All because you're not hitting your shot consistently solid. Once you can hit your putts solidly on a regular basis your focus needs to be on the speed of your putts.

Think of it this way. On every putt there is an optimum distance the ball should roll past the hole. The distance you hit the ball determines your percentage of possible makes. Dave Pelz did a test with a machine rolling ten foot putts which barely reached the hole. The machine made only about 50 percent of those putts. That percentage went up to about 90 when the speed on the ball was increased to where the putt would roll seventeen inches past the cup.

The conclusion is obvious. You'll make more putts if you hit them at a pace which would see the ball come to a halt about a foot or so past the hole. At least on relatively flat putts. Seventeen inches can turn into three feet pretty quick on a downhill or sidehill putt. Those putts are lag putts. Aim for the front lip on those.

But, generally speaking, putts need a little pace on them to hold the ball on line. If you "die" a ball at the hole, it will be moving slowly and be more susceptible to any imperfections in the green.

How much pace you give a putt depends on your situation and how good you are at controlling your speed. If you're not very good, roll the ball to the hole and no further. If you're good, roll your putts so that if they miss they will finish by the hole.

Reading the Breaks

When you have determined how hard you want to hit a putt, that calculation also determines where you should aim (see fig. 107). You need to get both pace and line correct if you want to make a putt. I see amateurs spending a lot of time on the greens trying to figure out how much putts are going to break. Then they hardly consider how hard they are going to hit the ball. How much break you play is always related to how hard you hit a putt. The harder you hit the ball, the less it will break. The softer you roll the ball, the more break you have to allow. As a general rule, most golfers don't play enough break. Statistics say that around 85 percent of all putts are missed on the low side of the hole and, for once, I believe the numbers.

You need to play four to six times more break than you think. That sounds like a lot, but it is a fact. Next time you are over a breaking putt consider that, even though you think you are playing enough borrow, so did 85 percent of the people who had this putt before you. And they missed it low. So play more than you think! Try to beat the odds. You have a better chance of making it from the high side than the low. The ball won't drop in from below the hole. That's why the low side is called the amateur side.

The more break you play, the better you are going to do with your speed. During the 1995 Masters Tournament CBS announcer Peter Kostis made a great observation on how Ben Crenshaw was handling

FIG. 107 Every holed putt is a combination of perfect pace and perfect line.

the fast greens at Augusta. He commented that Ben always plays the maximum amount of break on his putts. Allowing for the maximum break forces you to focus on your speed. Crenshaw does both and no one could deny that he has made his share of putts over the years. Whenever you aren't playing enough break you will instinctively hit the ball harder to keep it on line. That's when the ball can get away from you. On fast greens especially, always play the maximum amount of break. That way, you can hit your putts as softly as possible.

Speed also determines how long your next putt will be. There is nearly always a next putt. No one makes everything. So you have to stand over every putt considering—at least a little bit—your next putt. That's not negative, just realistic.

Dare yourself to play enough break. Putts either break a little bit, or a lot. But always more than you think. And every green has some slope to it, at least a half inch for every ten feet. That's the way architects design putting surfaces—so that they drain properly. There is no such thing as a flat putt. You may have a straight putt, but if so it is uphill or downhill.

If you are standing on a perfectly flat green, you are standing on a dead green. The best way to read a green is to look for where the water drains off it. Sometimes it'll be off the front, sometimes off the side, sometimes off the back. Greens are designed to get water flowing off of them. If you dumped a big bucket of water on the green, where would it go? That's where the ball goes, too.

Make Every Putt Straight

Let's pause for a moment. The last few paragraphs will have hopefully made you think more about your putting. Which is good. But don't go too far. Don't go thinking that putting is a complicated and difficult process. It isn't. Keep things simple.

For example, you don't "work" the ball in putting. You can't hit hooks and slices. So every putt is essentially straight, no matter how much break there may be. Think about it. Even if you have a thirty-foot putt with a six-foot break on it, you still have to pick a point where you want the ball to start. You don't have to worry about the borrow, only your "target."

Pick your breaking point and start the ball there. Focus only on that. Let gravity do the rest for you.

Pre-Shot Routine

Just as in the full swing, a consistent pre-putt routine can instill a feeling of comfort and confidence once you are over the ball. "Sameness" is good.

Approach the ball from behind. Visualize the roll of the ball over the green, all the way to your aiming point. Then set your putter down, placing your feet perpendicular to the line. An open stance is also okay. Bobby Locke, one of the greatest putters ever, stood closed. But I like the orthodoxy of a square stance. If you are looking for consistency, it is nearly always best. Reinventing the game can be risky. Keep it simple.

Some Do's and Don'ts

FIG. 108 Address the ball with the toe of the putter up . . .

FIG. 109 or flat . . .

FIG. 110 but never with the heel up.

FIG. 111 In putting, your hands should be ahead of the ball at address . . .

FIG. 112 or over the ball . . .

FIG. 113 but never behind the ball.

FIG. 114 Your stance should be square when you putt . . .

FIG. 115 or open . . .

FIG. 116 but rarely closed.

FIG. 117 While putting, your eye-line should be over the ball . . .

FIG. 118 or inside the ball . . .

FIG. 119 but never outside the ball.

FIG. 120 Your head should be over the ball as you address a putt . . .

FIG. 121 or in back of the ball . . .

FIG. 122 but never forward of the ball.

FIG. 123 Your stroke should be straight back . . .

FIG. 124 or inside the line . . .

FIG. 125 but never outside the line.

CHIPPING

Hit Down

This is a simple shot. Most of your thought should go into your setup. Everything in your address position must be designed to keep the ball down and ensure you get a solid ball/turf contact.

Always play a chip shot back in your stance—back of center—no matter what club you are using (see fig. 126). Your stance should be open, your shoulders square, your hands forward. Your weight must be almost entirely on your left side. Your right shoulder is higher than on a normal shot. That pushes the center of your body forward. A line drawn up the middle of your body will be a couple of inches in front of the ball.

FIG. 126 Put the ball back in your stance to chip.

Stand very close to the ball (see fig. 127). Choke down on the club. Using your reverse overlap grip, keep your wrists and your hold on the club firm. Set the club upright, a little bit on the toe. Make a swing with your arms, similar to a long putting stroke but firmer and with more of a downward hit. Contact the ball then the turf, but don't make much of a follow-through. You are, after all, trying to hit a shot that comes out low and rolling.

FIG. 127 When chipping, stand close to the ball.

Pick Your Spot

When you can't putt, you chip. But whenever you can putt from off the green, do it. Even if you see the pros chipping from the fringe or

FIG. 128 Always choose a spot where you want your chip shot to land.

close to it. They are trying to eliminate the possibility of a bad bounce on the uneven ground between them and the green. But, generally speaking, a putt is a higher percentage play. Hence the phrase "a bad putt is as good as a good chip" is one of golf's more enduring clichés.

When you do have to chip, do what the pros do. They always try to land a chip shot on the green if they can, and so should you (see fig. 128). Predicting the bounce and roll of the ball is so much easier.

First, choose the spot where you want the ball to land. Always make it a safe distance on the green. Avoid contact with the fringe. A couple of feet onto the putting surface is usually fine, unless something like a wet spot or some rough grass or a hump tells you otherwise.

Which Club?

With any chip you want the minimum amount of air-time and the maximum amount of ground-time. Get the ball rolling as soon as you can.

I teach chipping with four clubs: 6-iron, 8-iron, pitching wedge, and sand wedge. Given that you are always aiming for the same spot on the green, one of your four clubs will nearly always produce the right amount of roll to the flag.

When the 6-iron would roll too far, use the 8-iron. When the 8-iron rolls too far, use the pitching wedge. When the pitching wedge goes too far, use the sand wedge. When the sand wedge goes too far, hit a pitch shot.

If your ball lands on the spot you aimed for and rolls too far, you used the wrong club. If your ball lands on your spot and comes up short, you used the wrong club. You need more or less loft to make the ball roll the right distance.

If you chip with one club all the time, things get complicated. I see people trying to make one club work from anywhere. That's too difficult. It requires so much feel to make the same club hit the ball all those different distances. Most of us just aren't capable of that. Your landing point has to change with every shot. And you have to manipulate the shot and the club to produce the correct trajectory. That's too many techniques, too many spots.

The factors that determine which club you use are the speed of the green, the distance between your landing spot and the pin, and how far you have to carry the ball to your landing spot.

For example, if you chip a ball from three feet off the green and another from six feet off, the second ball is going to go further. You had to hit it harder to get it to the green, so it will roll more. So you need to use a more lofted club.

10

The Finishing Touches
Troubleshooting

In reality this final chapter could go on forever. Because golf is played outdoors and not on a flat surface, there are any number of shots and situations which fall under the heading "troubleshooting."

Indeed, that is one of the things which throws you off on the golf course. You spend hours practicing on a flat range, then get to the first hole and are faced with a shot from, say, a downhill lie you haven't worked on at all. Golf is like that. The Scots are right: It isn't meant to be a fair game.

Don't worry though. Things aren't so bad. In fact, any adjustments you make should nearly all be made at address—not in your swing. Certainly for uneven lies.

When the ball is in an awkward position in relation to your feet, all you are really trying to do is create an address position from which you can make your regular swing, or at least something close to it. Realize that sometimes the lie will cause your swing to be shaped a certain way, which in turn will cause a certain ball-flight. Allow for that.

For example, if the ball is below your feet, it will tend to fade. So aim left. A ball lying above your feet will tend to draw. So aim right. In other words, the ball will fly with the slope. Don't fight it. You'll lose that battle. Go with the lie, in terms of the flight it will create.

Then there is an uphill lie, your back foot lower than your front foot. The ball will again follow the slope, way up in the air. Downwind, that can add distance to your shot; upwind the height on the shot will hurt you distance-wise. So you must adjust your choice of club to accommodate either or both.

The same is true on a downhill lie. The ball will again follow the slope, this time flying lower than normal.

The common factor on any and all of the above situations is that you want to get as close as possible to your normal setup position. In other words, you must align your body with the slope in order to create the same body angles you employ on a shot from a flat lie.

But we're getting ahead of ourselves. In this chapter I am not going to attempt to cover every possible situation and lie. That would be impossible anyway. Instead, I will cover the most common uneven lies, problem shots, and misconceptions I see causing my students problems. Here we go.

WHAT NOT TO THINK ABOUT

As I told you at the start of our opening chapter, I ask many questions early in a lesson with a new pupil. Here's another.

"What do you think about during your swing?"

The answer or answers tell me a great deal about any misconceptions a student may have about the golf swing in general and his own particular method. If he is like most golfers he will have at least a slightly confused view of what is right and wrong in his swing.

You know what I mean. You get well-meaning advice from your Saturday morning four-ball partner. You hear so-and-so on television. And you watch others swinging. All that information gets stored away—golfers will try anything and listen to anyone—until it comes out in an incomprehensible rush.

The temptation is great, I know. But forget these so-called shortcuts to success. In my experience they simply don't work. So clear your head of all the nonsense you hear on the first tee and in the grill room. Forget all those silly clichés like "keep your head down," "swing slow," and "make a full turn."

Simply throw them away. You'll play much better with one clear swing thought or an overall feeling or picture of what your swing should feel like and look like. No one can cope with much more than that. The club and your body are moving too fast during the swing. Your mind simply can't keep up.

So let's move from confusion to clarity. Let's get rid of the stuff you don't need to think about. Then you'll be free to focus on the important stuff.

"Keep Your Head Down"

I'm not sure who first came up with this totally erroneous piece of advice, but I hope he's somewhere no golfer can find him. The only thing keeping your head down achieves is a restricted swing (see fig. 129). Actually, that's not true. If you keep your head down after you've hit the ball—poorly no doubt—you'll also restrict your follow-through.

Do either or both and you'll put strain on your back because you will be forced to tilt rather than turn your shoulders. And that will surely knock your swing off plane. You'll swing too steeply and rarely hit the ball solidly.

You can avoid that tortured scenario by starting at address with your head up, not down. The back of your neck and your spine should form close to a straight line (see fig. 130). From there you can make an unrestricted turn of your shoulders under your chin, both on the backswing and the through swing (see figs. 131a and 131b).

FIG. 129 All keeping your head down does is restrict your swing.

FIG. 130 At address a line drawn down your neck and back should be close to straight.

And don't forget to let your eyes come up after you've hit the ball. I always tell my students that if they hit a good shot they should enjoy it, and if they hit a bad shot they've got to go find it. So let your head come up after impact and have a look at the ball.

"Keep Your Left Arm Straight"

After "keep your head down," this is usually the second piece of advice every struggling golfer receives. Unfortunately, the tendency most people have is to exaggerate the feeling. All too soon, "left arm straight" turns into "left arm stiff." Or "rigid." Or "tight." Or "tense."

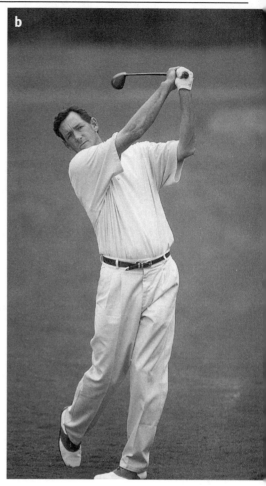

FIG. 131 Your left shoulder moves under slightly on the backswing (a), then your right shoulder moves the same way on the through swing (b).

Whatever the terminology, the end result is the same: your arms are prevented from swinging freely. Any tightness or rigidity limits your ability to make a fluid, rhythmic swing. And if your left arm is so tense that the forearm cannot rotate properly on the backswing, chances are your swing is going to be equally restricted.

So, instead of "straight," think "soft." Even if your arm does tend to bend a little on the backswing, don't worry about it. The force of your downswing will straighten it anyway. A soft left arm allows you to swing freely and is an important part of any fluid, fast swing.

"Shift Your Weight"

In the golf swing there are causes and there are results. Transferring your weight properly in the backswing is one of the latter. It isn't something you should focus on particularly. If you make a correct pivot it will happen all by itself as if by magic.

And what is a correct pivot? Think shoulders. You need to get both shoulders behind the ball at the top of your backswing.

How does that feel? Adopt your address position, then hold a club across your chest. Turn your shoulders until the shaft is over your right foot (see figs. 132a and 132b). That's how your turn should feel.

FIG. 132 To practice your turn, place a club across your chest (a), then turn until the shaft is over your right foot (b).

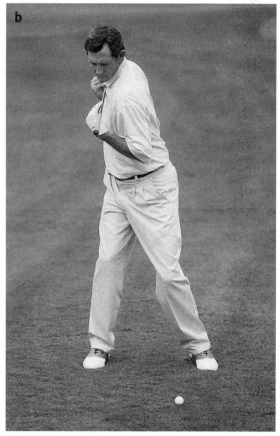

"Make a Bigger Turn"

One source of extra distance—always a temptation—is making a bigger swing (see fig. 133). The longer your arc, the more clubhead speed you will be capable of producing—if you create that length properly, of course. Here's how.

As I said in chapter Three, your hands start in front of your body. All you have to do is keep them there. Or get close to it. When your hands are still "within" the width of your body and your wrists are fully cocked, you will have stored up a great deal of potential energy, all of which you will be able to unleash through the ball (see fig. 134).

FIG. 133 A big arc doesn't necessarily mean more distance.

FIG. 134 Keep your hands and arms "within" or in front of your body.

"Swing Slowly"

Timing is a sometimes underestimated aspect of the golf swing. It's so important that you swing at a pace you can comfortably handle. That way, you can get your hands, arms, and body working in sync.

Trouble is, I see as many players swinging too deliberately as I see swinging too hard. All because they have this misguided notion that it is possible to swing too fast. It isn't. As long as you maintain your balance, you can swing the club as fast as you like.

Here's what to focus on instead. Think "smooth" rather than "slow." And within that constraint, go for it. No, make that really go for it. You heard me. Swing the club as fast as you can without falling over (see fig. 135).

It makes sense even if you have a poor swing. Remember what I said earlier? If you take a bad fast swing and slow it down, what are you left with? You got it. A bad slow swing.

FIG. 135 You can swing as fast as you can—as long as you keep your balance.

"Take the Club Back Low to the Ground"

Both you and the golf club should swing back to the inside in the takeaway, but in order to be on the correct plane the club must swing up as well. If you try to keep the club low to the ground early in the swing, it will end up under the correct backswing plane and likely loop over the top of the plane on the downswing.

So when should the club swing up in the backswing? Immediately but gradually. It should be coming up as soon as it starts back from the ball. But it should be moving around and up at the same time.

Okay, we've cleared your head a little. Let's talk about all those uneven lies.

UPHILL

This isn't as hard as it sometimes looks. Stand to the ball and try to line your shoulders up parallel to the slope. Even though the ground is uneven you want to be standing level in relation to the slope. Just like you do on the range. There you stand more or less level to the horizon. Here you can't do that. So stand level to the ground you are standing on (see figs. 136a and 136b). That's the key.

FIG. 136 When your front foot is higher than your back foot, keep your shoulders parallel to the hill (a), then swing "up" the slope (b).

The club swings down the slope, then back up the slope. Because of the uphill lie, the loft on the club is increased and the ball flies higher than normal. And you are going to have a hard time turning through the shot. Most of your weight will be on your right foot at impact. That can lead to you losing your balance, if only a little. Don't let that concern you.

Any time your body doesn't turn through and your hands keep going, there is going be a tendency for the ball to hook. Allow for that.

DOWNHILL

The same principles here. Align your shoulders with the slope, your weight focused this time primarily on your left foot. Make sure that stays the same through impact. Because the ball will tend to come out low, it's easy to fall back in a usually futile attempt to increase loft on the club. Don't concern yourself with that. You'll probably end up hitting behind the ball. Go with what the slope gives you. The launch angle is given to you. Note also that a fade will naturally fly pretty high and so is easier to play off a downhill lie. The slope will tend to accelerate the turning of your body through the shot and so keep the clubface open longer. Don't get too greedy, however. Take enough loft to get the ball up in the air, even if it means you can't reach the green (see figs. 137a and 137b).

BALL ABOVE FEET

This situation naturally produces a flatter swing plane. Stand taller. Your posture has to change to find the angle between the ground and your spine that allows you to hit the correct amount of turf. Take a few practice swings to find proper setup and ball position.

The flatter your swing gets, the more your club will swing on an arc, and the more the ball will tend to hook. It will also fly lower.

If the ball is way above your feet, choke down on the club and stand closer. That will reduce your arc and the inside-to-inside swing shape. Focus on turning and allowing your arms to swing more around with your body. Aim right with the same club you would normally take for the distance. (see figs. 138a and 138b).

FIG. 137 On a downslope, your shoulders should parallel the hill at address (a), which enables you to swing "down" the hill (b).

FIG. 138 With the ball above your feet, stand closer, grip down on the club, and aim to the right (a). Then think "around" on the backswing (b).

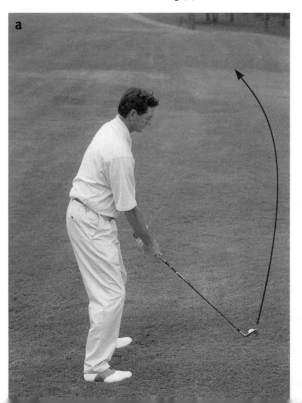 

BALL BELOW FEET

Bend over more from your hips. The mistake I see people making is bending from the knees. If you do that you'll straighten up through impact. Instead, get more angle from your spine and place less emphasis on the turning motion and more on just swinging the club up and down with your hands and arms. That's a straighter swing, which will cause the clubface to open. So a slice is likely. When that is the case, aim a little left (see figs. 139a and 139b).

HIGHER

We've all been here. You've got a free swing but you have to get the ball up quickly over a tree or some other obstacle, then stop it just as quickly on landing.

FIG. 139 With the ball below your feet, bend over more from the hips and aim to the left (a). Then think "up" on the backswing (b).

FIG. 140 When you want to hit a really high shot, set up with the ball forward in your stance (a). Then hang back on your right side and "scoop" the ball with your hands through impact (b).

So what do you do? You hit down to make the ball go up, right?

Wrong. Very wrong. "Hit down to make the ball go up" may just be the most misleading idea ever in golf. Two things make the ball rise—loft and spin. Spin comes from the speed you swing the club at. Loft you can increase by moving the ball forward in your stance, placing more weight on your right side, and moving your hands back behind the ball.

Even then, you need a decent lie. You need something under the ball because you will tend to bottom out behind it and hit the shot fat or thin. If I had to go over a tree, I'd always hope I had a good lie so that I could hang back on my right side and scoop the ball up with my hands (see figs. 140a and 140b).

In contrast, hitting down makes the ball go down. Hitting down delofts the club.

LOWER

If you are playing an approach shot into the wind make a shorter swing. A three-quarter swing at three-quarter speed will automatically produce a lower ball-flight. How much more club you need depends on the strength of wind.

Turn your left wrist down through impact. There should be a feeling of the back of your left wrist bowing, the knuckles turning down. Break the momentum of your swing by allowing your arms to relax and recoil back into your body as you feel the extension with your hands. Finish lower, too, your swing abbreviated. The lower the shot, the lower and shorter your finish should be (see figs. 141a, 141b, and 141c).

If you are trying to play a really low shot under a tree limb or into a Scottish-strength wind, or if you are looking to advance the ball as far down the fairway as you can, go with the following approach.

Place the ball back in your stance. Put most of your weight on your left side. Once set at address, hit down more on the ball. It will fly like a knuckleball. That's more effective when you don't need to control your distance. It also isn't so good when you are trying to land a ball on a green and make it stop quickly.

DOWNWIND

Good players hit lower shots downwind. If you hit hard with the wind behind you it gets difficult to judge just how far the ball will fly and run on landing. A lower ball-flight helps with both, which is why tour pros often use a three-quarter swing with the wind behind them.

ELIMINATE DISASTERS

Those are the basics when it comes to problem shots. I find that most people can make at least a half-decent attempt at any or all of them. They aren't really what drive up scores. Big numbers typically stem from inconsistency and the occasional disaster.

Not many high-handicappers have consistent games. Which is why they are what they are, of course. A typical 18-handicapper doesn't shoot 90 by making eighteen bogeys. No, he makes a bunch of pars, maybe a few bogeys, then has at least a couple of disasters.

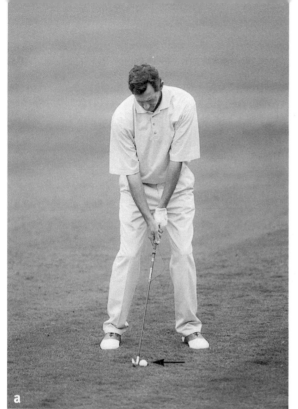

FIG. 141 To hit a really low shot, position the ball a little back in your stance (a), extend the club low through impact (b), and curtail your follow-through (c).

Those high numbers on a hole are what you need to avoid if you want to get your handicap down. And I know, that is easier said than done. Triples and quads don't result from the occasional missed fairway or green; they follow shots that are so bad a big number is inevitable.

You know what I mean. The popped-up drive. The big slice or hook out of bounds. Topping an approach into the lake in front. Shanking. Duffing a chip or two. Thinning a pitch shot.

I hope not all of the above applies to you, but if some of those sound too familiar, take some time to fix them. It's worth a little effort. We're not talking about a major reconstruction of your swing here, only fixing what can be expensive problems. It can only be worthwhile.

THE POP-UP DRIVE

This shot can only stem from you hitting down on the ball too much, the club coming into the ball on too steep an angle. Do that with the ball teed up and it hits too high on the clubface or right on top of the club. If you hit the ball on top of the club you are actually hitting with ninety degrees of loft. When that happens, the ball rises. And rises.

First, check the height you have the ball teed at. Only about half of the ball should show above the top of the club at address (see fig. 142).

FIG. 142 Only half of the ball should be above the head of your driver at address.

That's the easy part—now you have to work on flattening that swing out a bit. Set up to a ball as you would normally, then straighten your back until you are standing almost upright. The clubhead will be about two feet above the turf.

Now make some practice swings as if hitting a baseball. Feel as if the club is more over your right shoulder as opposed to over your head at the "top." Then swing the club back to "address." Again focus on turning your shoulders level and swinging the club on a more level plane (see figs. 143a, 143b, and 143c).

Once you have a feel for that move, keep going to the end of your follow-through. Repeated often enough, this little exercise will reduce the steepness in your action and, in turn, your drives. They'll soon be flying forward rather than up.

TOPPED FAIRWAY WOOD

You can top a shot with any club, of course, but I see it more often with fairway woods than any other.

There are three types of topped shots: A "miss-radius" top, a "steep" top, and a "shallow" top (see figs. 144a, 144b, and 144c).

A miss-radius top is often caused by a loss of posture. Typically, I see players losing the forward bend they have from their hips. Which is usually an attempt to compensate for an overly steep swing. Once you have a good posture at address, maintain it by keeping your rear end out during the swing.

A steep top usually ends up as a "grounder" to the left as the club comes straight down into the ball from the outside. The club just doesn't have an opportunity to get to the back of the ball. An inside takeaway is invariably the prelude to this shot, followed by the outside loop which causes the steepness into impact.

Take some practice swings where you try to reverse your loop. Feel the club swinging more "under" at the start of the downswing, then more up and to the right through impact.

A shallow top is just the opposite. It usually travels straight or to the right and is caused by the club approaching the ball on too flat an angle to make solid ball-turf contact likely.

In other words, the club is too close to the ground too far from the ball. When that happens you will catch the ball on the upswing instead of at the bottom of the arc.

The causes are an arm swing that is too flat, a shoulder turn that's too level, or dropping the club in behind you and too much to the in-

FIG. 143 To correct the "pop-up" drive or the "steep" topped shot, make a more level swing, get the club above your right shoulder at the top (a), re-create "address" (b), then swing the club around the finish (c).

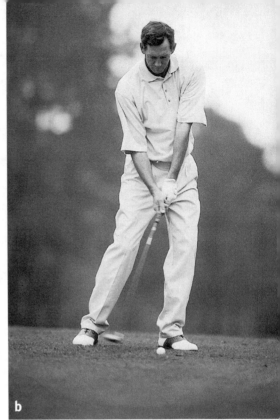

FIG. 144 The "pull-up" top (a), the "steep" top (b), and the "shallow" top (c).

side on the downswing. The correction is a little steeper shoulder turn or arm swing and better rotation of your left arm down and into your body at the start of the downswing. That gets the club more out in front of you so that it can approach the ball on the correct angle and produce a solid hit.

FAT SHOTS

Although every fat shot is caused by the bottom of the swing occurring behind the ball, there are different ways to hit a shot fat. Your swing can be too steep, the club digging into the ground. Your swing can be too shallow, the club contacting the ground before it gets to the ball.

Steep-Fat

If your iron shots are fat and your divots are deep, you know your swing is too steep. So you need to flatten your swing out, maybe by making a more level shoulder turn. Or you might need to get your arms and the club on a flatter plane on the downswing—not just on the takeaway. A flatter start to the swing can easily lead to you looping the club over the top on the way down, which steepens your swing even more.

Focus first on your shoulders. Try to turn them level, or at least what feels level to you. And try to swing your hands and arms around your body as opposed to straight up and down. Make a few swings with the club held a few inches off the ground. That will encourage the feel you are looking for.

Shallow-Fat (1)

Here, your swing is too flat. Maybe your turn is too flat, or maybe your hands and arms are swinging on too flat a plane.

Try to get your hands and arms swinging the golf club more up and down in the backswing, the downswing, and the through swing. Emphasize the turning of your hips on the downswing and the through swing. This helps bring the bottom of the swing forward to the ball.

Shallow-Fat (2)

Better players can also hit the ball fat when the club is approaching the ball from too far behind them. That can stem from too upright a backswing leading to an excessively flat downswing, or maybe the player fights a hook by dropping the club inside on the downswing in an effort to stop the ball going left.

Emphasize the rotation in your left arm on the backswing. From the top of your swing, feel your arms dropping and your left arm rotating into your body. It's the same kind of correction you would use for fixing a hook.

The Shank

This is a horrible shot, more of a disease than a poor shot. It happens when the club is swung too much out in front of you through impact. The hosel hits the ball, which rockets off to the right.

There are four main causes of a shank, but the common factor is that the clubhead is swinging out too far from your body on the downswing. It is reaching out more than it should. The question is: why?

1. You could be standing too close to the ball. Which, of course, is easily corrected (see fig. 145).
2. You could be getting closer to the ball (leaning in) during your swing. In other words, falling into the shot. The symptom is a feeling of being off-balance toward your toes (see fig. 146).

    Make sure you keep your left shoulder "up" as it turns in the backswing. And keep your head back, away from the ball. Forget any thought you had about keeping your head "down." That can only make your problem worse.
3. You could be swinging your hands and arms on too flat a plane (see fig. 147a). That puts the club too far behind you on the backswing, too far in front of you on the through swing.

    Swing the club more up and down with your hands and arms, and keep the club more in front of you going back (see fig. 147b).
4. You could simply be reaching out with your arms on the through swing (see fig. 148). Which, again, has a simple fix. Just try to keep your arms close to your body as you swing the club through impact.

So the first step in fixing a shank is analyzing which of these four variations you are prone to. Once you figure out which one you have, work on the correction.

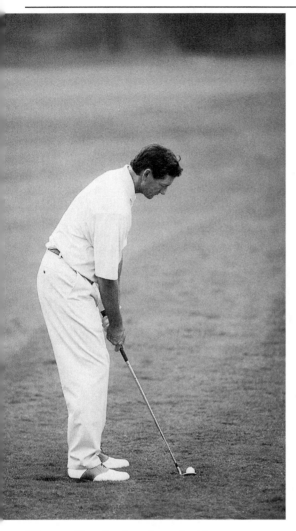

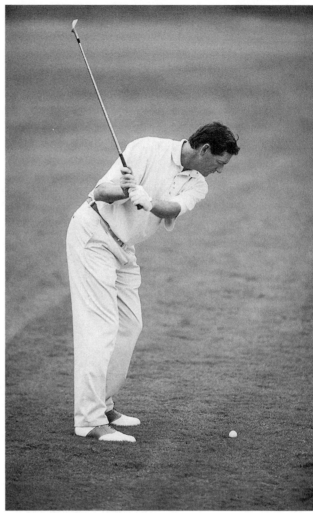

FIG. 145 Standing too close at address can cause a shank.

FIG. 146 Falling toward the ball can also cause a shank.

FIG. 147 Too flat a swing will cause a shank (a), as will reaching your arms too far toward the ball (b).

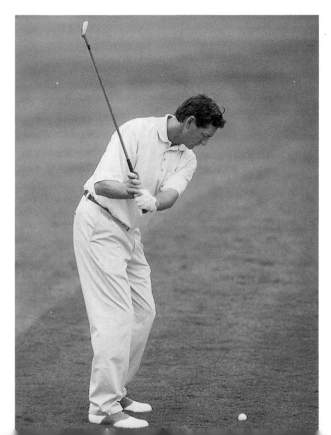

FIG. 148 To fix a shank, stay the correct distance from the ball and swing the club more up and down.

This little exercise will help with all four. Set up with a line of tees in the ground just outside the ball (see fig. 149). Make it your goal not to hit the tees. If you don't, you won't shank.

FIG. 149 Set up with a line of tees outside the ball—if you miss them you can't shank.

THINNED PITCH

Bad thinking or fear is often partly the cause of this destructive shot. But it starts when either the bottom of the swing is too far behind the ball or when you are lifting up through impact. You rise up in anticipation of hitting behind the ball and hit the shot thin instead.

One way to lift up is by "scooping" with your hands. That stems from a closed clubface negating the loft on the club in the backswing, then trying to add loft at impact. Fixing the problem takes some courage and a change in your technique.

Swing back, opening the clubface as you go. At the end of your shortened backswing the toe of the club should be pointing skyward, the back of your right wrist almost flat.

Let your arms swing down and feel your hips move forward and turn a little. That will encourage your weight onto your left foot,

FIG. 150 No hands—slide the club under the ball for the soft pitch.

which in turn will bring the bottom of the swing forward and help create a slight downward hit through impact. Forget hand action. By keeping the clubface open, you get the ball up quickly (see fig. 150).

FAT SAND SHOT

Short, jabby swings cause the problem here. And combined with a lack of understanding over how a sand wedge is designed to work, the result is you taking more than one shot to get out of a bunker. Not good.

There are three steps to this "fix." First, open the clubface. That will stop the club from digging into the sand. You want the flange to slide through the sand, not the leading edge to dig into it.

Second, make a full backswing as if you are hitting a medium iron (see fig. 151). Again, that takes courage at first. But practice builds trust.

Third, really accelerate the clubhead through the sand and into your follow-through (see fig. 152). Do that and the ball will definitely come out. I personally guarantee it. Even if you hit a little too far behind the ball, the extra momentum in the clubhead will throw the sand and the ball onto the green.

FIG. 151 To make sure you get out of the sand, make a full backswing.

FIG. 152 And a full follow-through.

CHUNKED CHIP

This is just a mini-fat shot. I see two common reasons for it. Players either make a downswing that is too much from the inside, or they think that the body must stay rigidly still during a chip shot. Neither is helpful.

Set up with your weight forward, on your left side. Really lean into your left foot to get your center forward and your hands and body ahead of the ball (see fig. 153). Simply shoving your hands forward

FIG. 153 To create a downward hit for a chip shot, lean into your left foot.

isn't enough to create the steeper angle of descent you need to hit this shot crisply.

Now swing the club straight back and through (see figs. 154a and 154b). Similar to a putting stroke, you must keep your hands out of this shot. Bumping your hips forward as you swing to the ball and turning your left hip through a little also helps you contact the ball first.

FIG. 154 A chipping stroke is straight back (a) and straight through with firm wrists (b).

Index